ONE AND ONLY

Learn about genuine self-love, grow your self-confidence, self-awareness, self- discipline. Achieve emotional balance with self-acceptance. Overcome low self- esteem and insecurity.

MELANIE SMITH

TABLE OF CONTENTS

INTRODUCTION

The ultimate goal of self-acceptance is to understand who you are in every aspect intrinsically and to accept yourself without recrimination or judgment.

To accept yourself is to be satisfied with yourself in every way possible. To truly understand yourself, you need to be fully aware of who you are. Your view of yourself will be understandable, as you are viewing yourself through your own eyes, though that is the only lens available to you. No one else's opinion of you matters as much as your own. How you view yourself is key that you like yourself is essential.

When you are self-accepting, you see all of your strengths and weaknesses, and you accept them as parts of you. You are the collection of thoughts, emotions, and physical traits that come together to define you. Mind, body, and soul, you define yourself.

Self-accepting is to let go of everything that held you back from taking control of your life and moving forward. You are free of shame and guilt, past limitations, and learned behaviors. Self-acceptance has given you forgiveness for the mistakes you made along the way and the ones you will continue to make as you move forward. It means you have overcome your upbringing's limitations on you, whether it be bad parenting or a lower-income environment.

Self-acceptance is self-validation. Self-validation is greater than validation from gaining value from other people's opinions of you. You have grown beyond the need to find approval and acceptance from external sources, such as your parents, friends, or boss.

Self-acceptance is not the same as self-improvement. To improve something is to make it better - to fix it. To repair something is to take elements of the thing being fixed and use them to finish the product. Self-acceptance is not about making you a better person or fixing you. You cannot take pieces of yourself and rearrange them. You are not broken; you are just in a different state. Self-acceptance is about discovering who you are and why you are the way you are and then embracing it. It is an affirmation of yourself, not a re- engineering of yourself.

Nor is self-acceptance the same as self-esteem. Self-esteem values only the good qualities you find within yourself, leaving the negative out of the conversation. Self-esteem focuses only on the positive aspects of who we are. With it, we appreciate only the positive qualities we find, leaving all the rest behind.

Self-acceptance embraces every aspect of our character. It does not pick, choose what to hold up to the light, and leave in the shadows. It shines a light on everything, holding it all up for the world to see, including the good, the bad, and the dark.

We all have a dark side - the place where we hide the scars and bury the hurt. Some refer to it as Pandora's Box, the deep well of dark secrets that haunt us - every ill-intended thought we ever had about ourselves and the world around us but never acted upon. No light can shine there, or so you would think. But the light of self-acceptance does. It has to, as self-acceptance is universal and all-encompassing. To value yourself and embrace every facet of who you are, you must come to terms and accept that this deep dark place plays a role in creating who you are, and you need to accept it as well.

There comes a time when you need to trust yourself. You dictate how happy your life will be. If you get to the point of self-acceptance, everything else falls into place. Look around you at confident people. They accept who they are, and many people can do this from a very young age. Those with secure backgrounds and who grow up with parents who can nurture them may never experience negative feelings about themselves. They may take for granted that everyone feels as they do. However, life isn't that simplistic. In a way, you have been through the worst stage of your life and have accepted that you need to do something about self-love. If you read all of the guides in this book, you will feel better about yourself and will have recovered from feeling negative. Negativity may have been the result of many years of self-criticism. Your positive approach to life from now on is necessary to override all negativity you have accepted as part of your life.

You can look at yourself in the mirror and see your true self. You are compassionate and kind and don't resort to things that diminish who you are. You know that negative emotions don't help you present yourself in a way that others easily accept. You also know that the responsibility for who you are is yours and no one else. Taking that responsibility in hand and realizing it's yours is a step in the right direction because your change of attitude means that you can cope with other people's negativity levels without making them rub off on you.

With all of the world in turmoil and with the pressures of life in the twenty-first century, your self-acceptance and love are the first turning points in your life that actually help you succeed and be happy. Stand on each stepping stone, and don't be afraid afterward. The water isn't that deep to drown you. Yes, sometimes, you get your feet wet, but that's a natural progression, and you learn from each mistake in life to tread more carefully in the future.

You are a precious human being with an entitlement to opinions of your own. You don't have to bow to the opinions of others. We have taught you how to deal with relationships and how to make relationships work for you. Your new positive attitude will help you to make friends. The fact that you have been on this journey of discovery means that you can see yourself as complete and don't need someone else to prop up who you are. That's wonderful news. Mr. or Mrs. Right won't be looking for broken people. They will be looking for whole people whose love for themselves allows them freedom of expression and positivity.

It is hoped that you come out of the other side of your negativity with strong self-love. People who love themselves don't leave themselves open to abuse. They encourage healthy, giving relationships. They present themselves as balanced and happy and capable of much more than they give themselves credit. Welcome to the world of complete people. Your days of working toward finding the best side of who you begin when you start to read the guides in this book to find that love for yourself and self-acceptance that all humans need.

If you understand this, you can realize what it truly means to achieve self-acceptance.

WHAT IS SELF-ACCEPTANCE?

———————— ⌒∽⌒ ————————

Unlike self-esteem, which is your personal evaluation of who you are, what you can do, where you can go, and your capabilities and values as a human being, self-acceptance is your ability to choose to affirm yourself. Acceptance is very different from perfection. When you accept something, you don't accept it because it's perfect. You just take it in rough spots and all. That is acceptance. It isn't done through some process where you have to be worthy or flawless first. Instead, look at yourself with all your imperfections along with all your potential. Learn to embrace the whole thing.

Not 90% or even 99.9% but the whole thing. You welcome all facets of what makes you who you are. Yes, this includes things that don't build up your self-esteem or go against the mental image you have of yourself. Self-acceptance is not a denial of your weaknesses or overlooking your shortcomings. It's a realistic appraisal of who you are, what you can be, and what you are capable of. From this estimation, you experience satisfaction. Despite your deficiency, you're far from perfect; you are satisfied with who you are. It is a core foundation for any solution to self-sabotage and other forms of self-harm.

Self-Acceptance Is Not Self-Improvement

People may say that self-acceptance goes against self-improvement. They think that there's a black and white difference between the two, and there's this thick wall that you can't go through. You have to pick one of the others. Self- improvement doesn't have to be the enemy. Please understand that you can't saddle yourself with this false dichotomy of choosing self-acceptance over self-improvement. Unfortunately, too many women believe this.

They think that if they accepted themselves, then they are basically lowering their standards. They're being complacent. They believe that they will stagnate because they will just accept themselves for who they are in the present, and what's the point of changing for the better? The confusion arises from the fact that you do so without the condition of "fixing" yourself when you practice self-acceptance. You just stay who you are right here right now, and you embrace it.

Even though you are aware of the different areas in your life that need repair, the self-acceptance is an affirmation of where you are currently. It is a necessary tool for self-improvement because you are no longer your own worst critic when you approve of yourself. It goes a long way in short-circuiting your normal tendency to undermine yourself, question your abilities, and otherwise engage in self-sabotage.

In other words, self-improvement is built on a foundation of confidence that can only come from self-acceptance. You get the energy that you need to make the necessary changes. You let go of this mental and emotional habit of always sniping at your efforts and your identity. With self-acceptance, you flip the switch, so you now have the focus and energy to work on what needs to be fixed, changed, or added to your life.

The Secret to Self-Acceptance

What is the secret to self-acceptance? We're going to walk through some steps below, but there is one overarching idea that you need to wrap your head around. You have to internalize this. Self-acceptance can only happen when you don't impose conditions. Embrace yourself right here right now with no constraints. Don't play this game with yourself where you say, "If I could only change this one part, I will accept myself." Get rid of those "if-then" statements.

Either you acknowledge yourself as you are, or you don't. It's that basic. There are no conditions for self-acceptance. Otherwise, you're just going to kick the can down the road, and tomorrow will never come. There will always be a flaw that you can notice, and if you are going to wait until those requirements are met, and things feel right, you're going to wait forever. Don't even start with that game.

The Steps to Self-Acceptance

Be your own best cheerleader. Source your motivation from the only place you can control. That, of course, is you. Many people run out of motivation because they make the mistake of picking other people or certain situations as their motivation source. It is where they fail. Bear in mind that you can't control those people. There's no guarantee that you can bring about specific circumstances or prevent them from happening. Why locate your origin of control and validation on things and situations you do not have charge of.

Concentrate on the conclusion that you're not as bad as you think you are because certain things in your life are going right. You can make things occur. Repeat this line, "I can make things happen." Repeat it several times. Once you've done that, believe it because that is the truth. If you have no job or you're struggling with a minimum wage positioned somewhere in Middle America as you read this, we can guarantee you there are hundreds if not millions of people all over the world who would love to be in your shoes right now. Things are going right. We know it may sound ridiculous to you but focus on the things that lead to where you are now. It's not all a catastrophe nor is your life one giant failure.

When you understand that, believe in yourself. Sure there are a lot of things going awry. Maybe your relationships are toxic, you're frustrated with your career or lack of one, or your finances worry you but focus on what you've done right. From there, fixate yourself on what you can do. You have tried and proven ability to do the right thing. If this makes sense, feel good about it. Blow it up in your mind, expand it.

When all you look at are your mistakes and failures, the bigger they become, they overshadow the rest of who you are. There's no complete and utter failure. At least, they got 1% right; otherwise, they won't be alive. So direct your attention to what you've done right and trust your skill to make the correct call.

Change Your Self-Talk

We all have this internal script that we keep repeating, and we have to be very careful since so many women engage in self-talk that holds them back and drags them down. Their self- talk makes them feel small, weak, powerless, voiceless, and marginalized. They repeat this cycle, and guess what happens? It becomes their reality. It's a form of self-hypnosis. When you concentrate on what you're doing right, you start believing in yourself because that's the proof you've been looking for.

Things aren't an absolute disaster because, at the very least, you can afford to read a book at a cafe. Life isn't as bad as it can be because nobody is stabbing you right now or blowing your brains out with a gun pointed at the back of my head. That's something to celebrate. So praise the choices that brought you to where you are and incorporate the fact that you can do things right despite the obvious negative consequences of other decisions. This realization starts to chip away at your low self-esteem or self-talk that makes you hate yourself by concentrating on your capabilities.

Reward Yourself with Positive Emotions

Now that you have interrupted your self-talk and replaced it with affirmations of your ability to make things happen, the other step is to reward yourself with positive emotions. Many women believe that it's not much of a reward because there's no price tag, you can't eat it, or there's no taste or no aroma. When you realize it, most of the big material prizes that we tend to focus on and obsess over are rewards only because they have an emotional impact on us.

When you view your empty task list for the day because you finished everything on it, zero in on the fact that you are a capable person; you were able to manage your time and focus on willpower in such a way that this list that had items that you'd instead not do is now clean. Concentrate that strong emotion of control, self-satisfaction, and victory. Allow yourself to compare yourself with who you were before. Think about the fear that you had and the annoyance that you felt. Contrast that with this feeling of relief and fulfillment. Before you know it, this contrast will be enough to motivate you to keep craving that same sense of achievement. Do it sufficient times, and it becomes part of who you are.

Embrace Your Weaknesses

If there is some authority you can exert on your weak spots, then go and take those steps towards self-improvement but never let your awareness of your weaknesses stop you from loving yourself fully right now, even if those changes that you've taken are long in coming. Accept your flaws so you can work around them so you can also bring focus on your strengths. Start redefining what your vulnerabilities are. They are just reminders of your strengths. They are not there to imprison you, nor are they marks of inferiority.

Focus on Progress, Not Perfection

It is the contrast between progress and perfection. You know that chances are, the first time you attempt something it's not going to meet your expectations, but you need to do it anyway. You can't play this game of expecting perfection from yourself, or else you won't act. That doesn't work. It doesn't even make sense, but it does have a strong emotional punch to it. It's illogical because for you to become perfect, you have to practice.

What does the practice take? That's right, action. So you have to show up and do what you have to do. The results may not be anything to write home about, but you just have to keep showing up. Eventually, you will be able to connect the dots, learn from your mistakes, and achieve a predictable level of results. That's how it works. Even if you are Michael Jordan and you have all this tremendous potential, if you just sit on your potential, nothing will happen. You have to practice.

Shift Your Personal Commentary to Celebrating Your Baby Steps

A lot of our personal commentary in our self-talk focuses on where our final destination is. It then compares where we are now with our final goal or desired final state, and what happens next? We feel lousy and ask ourselves, "What's wrong with me? What's taking me so long? So many women end up with the right guy; why can't I? How many frogs do I have to kiss before I find my prince?" Does this sound familiar? Now that you understand the difference between perfection and progress focus on the road ahead. Concentrate on the steps you're taking and less on the ultimate destination.

Before you know it, you arrive at where you need to go sooner rather than later. Re-shift your focus. Stop beating yourself up and sabotaging your journey by holding yourself up to an impossible standard or dwelling on ideals of perfection. Focus instead on how things are, and use your means to push you forward, not drag you down. There is a difference.

EVERYTHING STARTS WITH SELF-ACCEPTANCE

Now that we understand what self-acceptance is and how it works, we can move on to how it actually looks like in real life because everything starts with self-acceptance. You will know that you have achieved 100% self-acceptance when you can look at yourself in the mirror and accept everything about you literally. You are no longer trying to fix, ignore, or explain any 'faults' or 'flaws' that you may have.

Self-acceptance looks different for every single person. It all depends on what struggles we have gone through and what pieces of our lives we'd instead not acknowledge. Below are a few real-life examples of what self-acceptance looks like for other people:

A man going through a divorce feels like a complete failure because it may experience self-acceptance as realizing that he has made mistakes, and his marriage failed, but it does not make him a failure in general.

A person struggling with anorexia may accept themselves as a person with an imperfect body, understand that she approaches her imperfections in a harmful perception, and is committed to changing this perspective.

A student who works hard only to get mediocre marks in university could reach the point of self-acceptance. He realizes that studying and test-taking is not his strength and that this is alright because he has other strengths focus on.

A boy with low self-esteem who always ignores facing his self-defeating and self-doubting beliefs may experience self-acceptance by acknowledging his negative thoughts and realizes that not everything he thinks is necessarily true.

An employee struggling to meet goals set by an unreasonable boss may accept himself by accepting that sometimes he will fail to deliver during unjustified deadlines. However, he can still be a good person, even if he was unable to deliver.

Do you see the trends in these examples? Self-acceptance realizes that even though you are not perfect in one aspect of your life, it does not mean you are not valuable overall. Being self-accepting is allowing yourself to be bad at certain things and recognizing that you are good at other things. To have a healthy level of self-esteem, you have to be able to be self- accepting and accept certain things to be able to let it go. Holding on to every downfall, you may have been detrimental to a person's self-esteem.

Using Self-Acceptance in Therapy

Now that we learn a few examples of using self-acceptance in everyday life, one of its other main uses is therapy. Research has shown that lack of self-acceptance is directly related to lower well-being and even common mental illnesses like depression and anxiety. Suppose low self-acceptance causes low levels of mental and physical well-being. In that case, it may mean that higher levels of self-acceptance can act as a protective factor against these negative outcomes. The idea that self-acceptance is the foundation for healthy mental well- being is the driving factor behind; it also uses in therapy.

If you have ever gone to therapy, you have likely talked about the significance of being able to accept yourself and your reality. Your therapist probably helped you practice your ability to acknowledge the good and bad within you and accept all traits of yourself. However, one thing about self- acceptance is that to accept yourself fully and all of your weaknesses does not mean that you condone any bad behavior or accept harmful actions. You need to accept that you did engage in past bad actions, and you have undesirable traits, and those things are all part of who you are.

It is an essential difference to make and keep in mind because many people are confused with the idea that they must accept themselves when they have done something terrible. Accepting reality does not mean you like that reality. Do you see the difference? In the exact same way, accepting yourself and everything you do does not mean you have to like or celebrate every single aspect of yourself. Accepting the bad things about yourself is the most essential step in adapting or improving the things you don't like about yourself.

Using Self-Acceptance for Addiction Recovery

Self-Acceptance is a popular method to help people that are in addiction recovery. Acceptance is essential to those who abuse alcohol or other substances because they are often prone to using denial as a coping mechanism to avoid acknowledging their problems. They typically minimize, forget, rationalize, lie to themselves, or even repress memories or their abuse. While these coping methods may help some situations, it's not a good long-term solution to recover from substance abuse.

When an addict begins to recognize that they have a substance abuse problem, they may think that they can control all aspects of their lives simply because they want to change. It is a risky mindset because there are many things in our lives that we cannot control.

It is why self-acceptance is so vital in almost any kind of recovery process. Before you can make an essential change in your life, those who struggle with addiction must accept:

- The fact that they have a problem.
- The fact that they cannot control every part of their life.
- The fact that they have flaws and their own limitations.

- The reality of their situation.

Once the person has learned to accept reality and who they are, they can begin to work on changing the aspects that they can change. The purpose here is not to encourage self-blame but to change the purpose to something along the lines of ‚I don't like who I am right now, and I am going to help myself change.‘ Letting yourself to change for the better is the power of self-acceptance. You will then be able to fully be in reality and decide to help yourself instead of beating yourself up with blame and criticism.

NOTIONS OF GENUINE SELF-LOVE

Genuine self-love means that you accept that at this very moment, you are who you are, insecurities and all. You feel what you feel. Your genetic makeup is your genetic makeup. Your culture is your culture. When you truly accept your inner self, you will be showing love to yourself. Can you imagine the turmoil in loving half of who you are and hating or attempting to disregard the other half? That will set you up to search for your complete self in other people and sometimes dangerous external sources.

When you do not love all of yourself, you feel lost and incomplete, which explains the search for happiness outside yourself. However, when you fully love yourself, you can tap into all your internal resources and feel complete with or without other external sources. Genuine self-love means people, places, and things will be ancillary, and you will not feel like your world is ending when they change or leave.

You are in a healthy space when you want other people to be in your life but do not need them. Most people feel lost when they think that they are missing something or somebody they need to survive. We would suggest that what you need is an integrated relationship with your whole self and your higher power; however, you choose to define it. To prevent feeling strong attachments that seem to threaten your survival, begin to adopt the intentional statement, 'I'm good with or without x, y, or z.' Don't stop with the intentional statement. When you find yourself losing whatever you are attached to, begin engaging in behaviors that demonstrate that you love yourself, regardless.

We can fully love ourselves right now, today, bringing our

entire messy masterpiece into awareness, increasing compassion about our mess, and engaging in intentional and creative decisions that honor our entire self. Self-loving behaviors could include:

- engaging in a hobby, cooking, sewing, reading, writing
- exercising
- learning something new
- earning a degree, or
- meeting new people

Put simply; we can never really run away from ourselves. We might start living somewhere else or surround ourselves with a new group of people, but if you really want to be happy, then you've got to start by loving yourself. When it comes to self-love, you will soon realize that it is a process in itself, which usually follows five distinctive steps. These common steps or laws will make you understand how profound the concept of self-love can be. Understand the laws of self-love and commence your journey. Know where you are and take progressive steps to attain self-love.

Think Self-love

The first step would be around your thoughts. You need to make sure that you want self-love, and to attain it, you need to start practicing it. It is a known fact that we can change everything with our thoughts. Our thoughts gradually convert into our course of action. When you remind yourself daily about the need for self-love, the chances are that it will start reflecting on your actions.

To have such positive thoughts, you can recite mantras or practice meditation. It will help you to be closer to your inner soul, and you will start feeling more optimistic and spiritual from within. You can always start by writing journals and focusing on the good part of your life. Our world is consisting of good and bad, and it entirely depends on us which part we would like to experience.

They say that life is divided into two segments – the good and the bad. There is always a little bit of good in the bad and a little bad in the good. It is how life keeps its balance. Try to focus on the good half and think positive thoughts to take the first and the most crucial step towards attaining self-love.

Do Self-love

After being filled with optimism, you would need to vessel all that positive energy into your actions. Perform the kind of actions that would make you feel happy. Start by creating a healthy and pleasing environment around you. Our surrounding reflects our feelings in an unimaginable way. Try to find happiness in having less. Experiment with the minimalistic lifestyle as it will make you realize that less could be more at times.

Nurture a healthy and clean environment around you and get rid of the things you no longer want in your life. Go for walks and eat healthy meals to take care of your health. It is always a good idea to take yourself out for a meal every once in a while, but don't spoil yourself too much. Prepare healthy meals for yourself and treat your body like a temple. You are your physical manifestation and start taking care of your body to have a healthy and long life.

Start focusing on your lifestyle and do the things that make you happy. When you are in your action mode, get rid of all the negativity around you. Don't be lethargic and prepare an organized schedule for yourself. From waking up early in the morning to having meals at regular intervals, think of every possible thing while creating your schedule and stick to it at any cost.

We won't lie to you. The chances are that you might get tired and would even end up quitting in between. Every time you think you are losing it, do some meditation and clear your mind. Remind yourself why you are doing this and fill your body with just the right amount of energy to do self-love.

Absorb Self-love

Now when you have already started to love yourself, it is time to taste the fruits. This stage will come naturally when you would start falling in love with yourself. You might start buying things for yourself, but you need to make sure that you buy only the things that you essentially need in your life.

There will be a remarkable alteration in your lifestyle, and your loved ones might realize how you are becoming a happier individual. Everyone has a bucket list. If you don't have one, then come up with the things that you always wanted to do and complete it by doing one thing at a time. We will talk about the importance of bucket lists in a bit more detail shortly.

Instead of giving yourself any other materialistic thing that would come with an expiry date, gift yourself the kind of things that would last a lifetime. Enroll yourself in some class and teach yourself a new language or a musical instrument. Develop your passion and evolve yourself with time. It could be the best award that you can give to yourself.

Treat yourself with love while having a great time with your friends and family. Go out and travel somewhere alone, only to come home with some long-lasting memories. Treat yourself with some wisdom and make sure that you can grow yourself with every passing day. There are many ways to invest your time and other resources in yourself. Do it the right way so that you could be a better person in the long haul.

Surround yourself with positive people who influence you in a good way. When you place yourself in uplifting environments, you place yourself in a position to absorb more positivity and good feelings. Reposition yourself if your current environment and circle of influence do not enrich you until it does.

Retain Self-love

As you would start absorbing self-love, there might come a

time when you will start questioning your choices. Your life can get a little monotonous. It is time you take a leap of faith and do the most unimaginable things to be present with self- love.

When you are creating your schedule, you need to take some time off from your everyday activities for yourself. Never compromise on your time and give activities like yoga or meditation the same priority you give to your work. Take equal time for your passion and hobbies as well, and do what makes you happy. Don't be apologetic about it, as you are not doing anything wrong.

People might make you feel that you don't have time for them, but don't change your priorities to please someone else. Though, in the process, don't lose yourself and make enough time to sleep and relax. You must continue a regular sleep cycle and take proper rest to energize your body.

Don't create such a hectic schedule that you won't have time for yourself. Don't over-commit or make yourself so much busy that you forget to live in the process of doing the things you are supposed to do. Too often, people are not able to retain self-love as they just get tired. Only you can clear your priorities to choose love over anything else.

Exist in Self-Love

Realizing that self-love comes from within is one of the most insightful revelations you can have in life. It is your responsibility. That is why it is called ‚self-love.' One major method of loving yourself is to simply do it without regard to outward things or past experiences.

As long as you depend on something outside of yourself to give you a reason to feel or be loved, the process of actualization will be complicated—your sense of self-level rise and fall with the tides. In an unpredictable world, you must develop steady self-love that does not waver, or you will be tossed to and from upon the seas of life. Learn to exist in a state of self-love at all times, and you will build a shield around yourself that will deflect negative thoughts and radiate the light of an honorable inner life.

Feel Self-love

It might sound surprising, but self-love is not a destination – it is a journey that you need to take every single day. The last step is to make yourself feel self-love most unimaginably. It would start with physical touch as you would need to love your body and soul most purely.

You are now filled with love for yourself and can feel it in your bones. Do some exercise and stretch your muscles while feeling every inch of your body. You should be completely aware of who you are as an individual. You should know every part of your body and soul to love yourself.

Give yourself a facial or a spa treatment. Ensure that your hair plus nails are always prim and proper. Giving yourself a body spa or a scrub is undoubtedly a great idea. The more you feel self-love, the more fortunate you would feel. It would be the epitome of love and care, and you certainly won't let it go.

By this stage, you have experienced the true form of self-love. You have reached the pinnacle of self-love, and you would certainly never step down.

That was undoubtedly a fantastic journey. According to Buddha, no one in this entire universe deserves our love and affection than ourselves. These five laws of self-love are certainly proof of the power of self-love. Follow them wisely, and we are sure you would experience the most unadulterated form of love for yourself.

RADICALLY SELF-ACCEPTANCE

Lack of self-acceptance and chronically feeling inherently wrong are made exponentially worse when we face difficult life events. If you are going through a divorce or break up, or you're having difficulty with work or with the people you love in your life, then you may judge yourself more harshly than ever.

Feeling as if there is missing from your core means you don't see yourself as belonging to the larger whole, which brings on a crushing sense of aloneness. The lack of self-acceptance means you project onto others your disharmonious sense of self, and you are less likely to feel at ease with the people in your life. You may perceive that life is always hard. You can change this. Radical self-acceptance is the key to internal peace no matter what obstacles you face.

Feeling not good enough may have become such a robust mental habit that the neurons in your brain have acquired a hair-trigger when it comes to recalling negative stories about yourself.

One result of unrelenting self-criticism is a desperate need to feel better. In this situation, a person may turn anywhere in hopes of relief—unhealthy new relationships, an extraordinary effort to never be alone, sex without desire, compulsive achievement, constant attention to busyness, plastic surgery, dieting, material possessions—the list is long.

But at the same time, there persists a lingering and well-founded sense that these tactics will never really cure the problem because, after all, you can't really escape yourself. Engenders' hopelessness may lead to seeking relief through destructive behaviors—drug abuse, alcoholism, binge eating, not eating, shopping addiction, sexual addiction, hyper- consumerism— anything to feel better...if only briefly.

All human beings struggle with imperfection, and all human beings suffer; it's a component of human existence. Accepting this reality means that when you are suffering, you can just suffer instead of criticizing yourself for something that is a natural part of the human condition.

Habitually critical ways of interacting with yourself can be changed. If you are reading this book, you, along with most of humanity, struggle with self-acceptance. The first step in changing your mental wiring is to recognize how you have chosen to cope with this deficit. Come to terms with the behaviors you use (your "drug of choice") for medicating your self-esteem deficit, and recognize if you sponge off of others in a desperate quest to feel worthy.

Destructive Ways of Coping

For example: "For Jenna, it took all of her mental energy to get through the day and do what was required simply. She went through her work life with a stiff upper lip. As a professionally successful sales associate, she always puts on a happy face and an enthusiastic attitude. Even when sales fell, she would inspire her team, cheering them on to do better. She had a reputation around the office of someone who never let anything get her down. When she saw friends or family, she did not share much about herself but was ready to support them. However, Jenna crumbled when she was alone. Her friends, family, and work associates would never have recognized the alone Jenna. It was the complete opposite of the public-Jenna. She was deeply unhappy, aimless, and confused about what to do or how to deal with herself. Jenna so detested being alone that she worked herself to the bone all day and into the evening. She would prefer to see a friend on the way home from work or work until 11:00 p.m.—anything to avoid being alone with herself in her apartment. When she finally went home, she would numb her emotions by bingeing on junk food and zoning out watching TV until the wee hours of the morning. The only way she nurtured herself was with food. The morning after a binge, Jenna would harshly scold herself— "Stop binge eating or else!"—and then repeat the pattern that evening."

If you're experiencing low self-esteem, you may feel as if you're perpetually grinding your gears to get through the day. Addiction may beckon as a way to glide free for a short period—alcohol, drugs, sex, compulsive dating, the Internet, pornography, compulsive shopping. With so little self- nurturing, you search for a way to disconnect from yourself and the world around you.

Take an exact look at the destructive ways you cope with not feeling good enough. This analysis will help you come to terms with how much you need real care and nurturance.

Do You Sponge Off Others for Your Self- Worth?

If you struggle with chronic low self-esteem, then you are susceptible to looking for quick fixes to feel a modicum of value or worth. One particularly prevalent way to feel special and worthy is through the attention of others. The flip side of this is something I call the sponge effect. It comes when you are so desperate for the validation and approval of others that you become highly vulnerable to their negative emotions and reactions. You may soak up others' negative emotions or take on excess responsibility to please and keep others happy.

Also, suppose you compulsively depend on others to validate your worth. In that case, you may be susceptible to blaming yourself for the negative things that occur in your life— romantic rejection, work setbacks, or issues with friends—and fail to consider other more likely explanations.

You do not have a separate sense of self if your self-worth depends on how others treat you and what accolades you are receiving professionally or socially.

Recognize if you consistently farm out your worth to others. Notice how this makes you vulnerable because the whims and opinions of others are fickle and unsteady. Stop tuning into how others interact with you, and tune in to what's going on for you now. See how you experience yourself through your own eyes. What do you like, dislike, and need?

Instead of imagining what someone else might think of you, redirect your attention to your thoughts about what you need to be fully healthy. Observe when you feel a sense of internal peace, even if it's fleeting, or when you feel displeasure. If you are ambivalent, rather than just going forth or asking others their opinions, sit down and work through the ambivalence. Now let's turn to the work of helping you to connect with your worth separate from others.

Problem: "I don't know a better way."

Cure: Start a new relationship with yourself.

Whatever you are thinking within your head about yourself, allow it to be present with self-compassion and not self- criticism. When you unreservedly accept yourself, you will feel truly free and at ease; this leads to more intimacy with others, which provides a resilient buffer to all that ails you.

Being intimate with yourself means you accept yourself just as you are. Even when your emotions, actions, and reactions are painful, frustrating, or embarrassing, you hold onto these experiences with loving-kindness.

Becoming more intimate with yourself in this way will have a far-reaching impact, improving the quality of your romantic relationships and friendships, as well as enhancing your motivation and drive to get what you want out of life. Acceptance doesn't mean you do not want to change some aspects of yourself. Acceptance makes growth possible.

Humanizing Your Internal Critic

For many, an internal critic is always present and, at the same time, intangible. Carrying around this sense that "I'm not doing enough" or "Something is inherently flawed about me" means you can never quite be yourself with others.

For example, when Anya became more in touch with her internal narrative, she realized that every time there was a lull or pause in her day-to-day activity, her internal voice was telling her, "You're fat. You're so disgusting; no one wants you." Anya wouldn't allow herself to go to the gym out of fear that others would see her weight, pity her, and think, "Why is she working out? What's the sense?" She labored compulsively to avoid herself. Anya had no intimate relationships because she was terrified people would see all she hated about herself. At the same time, she was afraid to be alone because her internal critic attacked her. To compensate, when she found herself alone, she'd numb out with self- destructive behaviors.

Anya worked in therapy on becoming more aware of how she interacted with herself. She started to notice that her internal voice was consistently mean and punitive. She eventually drew a connection between the voice in her head and her mother, who was critical and dissatisfied with Anya throughout her childhood. She came to see how she picked up where her mother left off, mistreating and emotionally similarly abusing herself. At first, she had difficulty softening the voice in her head. Eventually, Anya was able to conjure up her father's voice, who had passed away years earlier. Each time she recognized her suffering, she imagined him saying, "You are worth it. You are strong and capable. I'm proud of you." Through her father's eyes, these three sentences and imagining herself began a process that inspired new thoughts about herself and allowed her to have new experiences.

Anya's consistency with this approach changed the way she interacted with herself. She became more accepting. She began to enjoy being alone, finally. She said it became the one time of the day "that I have no pressure from anyone to be a certain way or to take care of others. I'm free just to be me."

It's by looking at your experience straight in the eye—through reflection and self-observation—that negative elements lose their power. You will no longer have to live in fear of your internal experience and search for quick fixes or ways to camouflage, mask, or distract. Memories of negative experiences are no longer bad and scary. They can be present, and you can sit with them and reflect.

Now, if all you do is reflect, you may become self-critical again, so while reflecting, take a compassionate stance with yourself.

ACHIEVE EMOTIONAL BALANCE

Now that you are ready and willing to put yourself first, it is time to start transforming your emotional imbalances to balance. It is time to begin healing yourself, and it is time to walk the path to self-acceptance.

It Is Bad to Be Emotional

When you think of someone being emotional, do you see it as a positive or a negative? In most cases, people see it as a negative; if you know, this also causes you to see yourself negatively since you have been emotional your entire life. Take this moment to shift your perception about what it means to be emotional. Allow yourself to let go of any old beliefs or feelings that you have been holding onto or were instilled in you that make you feel bad or ashamed for being "too emotional" in moments when you were just yourself. At this moment, let go of any self-loathing feelings or thoughts and replace them with self-love and self-acceptance. Embrace being emotional as a positive and as a great gift and ability. From this moment forward, when someone says you are emotional or refers to you as being "too emotional" or "too sensitive," you can proudly reply with a "thank you." The more you embrace being emotional as a positive, the better you will feel, and the more you will be able to connect with your gift and abilities.

I Am Powerless Over What Happens to Me

The most important thing to realize in life is that you have power over what happens to you. By taking responsibility for your part, you will completely shift your reality and your perspective. How you think and feel internally creates what happens around you. Where you put your energy and what you allow in as part of your truth creates your perception; therefore, it is what you experience daily—this might be tough to hear or accept at first, but once you do, you will see and understand.

It is up to you if you are going to feed into the illness with which you were diagnosed or if you are going to see it as a learning experience from which you will benefit. If you choose to give way to it and let it become who you are, you will most likely suffer and be held back. If you see your illness as your body letting you know, it is time for some self-awareness and healing, that is precisely what it will be. If you had a terrible thing happen to you when you were a child and are thinking, "There is no way I contributed to that. I refuse to take responsibility for something I couldn't prevent and had no control over." We ask you to take a few minutes right now and see what came out of that incident. You might be startle by what you find. What you thought was terrible has now transformed into a blessing in disguise. You were "abandoned" by your biological parents and has now transformed into a gift you were given. It has turned into the first step that brought you to where you are today, which helped you become who you are along the way. It is up to you to decide if you will take responsibility and empower yourself from this moment forward, or if you are going continue to victimize yourself and live thinking and feel you have no power over what happens to you.

I Am Better and More Spiritually Aware Than Others

Several people misunderstand the meaning of putting yourself first and have gone to an extreme. They went from being selfless and self-sacrificing to selfish and self-centered in a negative way. To stay balanced, you must always remember to remain humble and come from a place of Love. Always remember you are not better or worse than anyone. Yes, you have a gift, but that does not make you more righteous. If you stay humble and always come from a place of Love, then you will stay balanced and happy and be very successful in everything you do.

Better to Give Than to Receive

It is a phrase that most likely resonates with you completely. Always wanting to give, give, give, but this is a big reason you find yourself out of balance and putting others' needs before yours. If you do not receive, receive, receive, then not only are you doing yourself harm because you give more than receive, but you are putting out to others that they matter more, and that is how you will be treated. By giving and not receiving equally, you are also not allowing someone else to experience the beautiful feeling of giving, especially giving to you. You are very loved because of your genuineness and compassion for others. Others want to give to you to thank you and show you how much they appreciate you. Allow others to show you how appreciative they are of you and how great they know you are by allowing yourself to receive with gratitude and ease.

I Am Not Worthy

If you look back at every situation in the past year where something did not work out in your favor, ask yourself in how many of those moments you felt you were not worthy enough and thought someone else was better than you in some way. If a relationship you were in did not work out, and you were devastated, look back and see why things did not work out. Now looking back, you realize you felt you were not worthy of your partner. If you did not feel worthy of them or your relationship, why should they want to stay? From this moment forward, always affirm to yourself that you are worthy, especially at the moment when you feel the opposite. Affirm, you are worthy of a healthy and reciprocated relationship. You are worthy of a successful career. You are worthy of a happy and peaceful home. You are worthy of everything your heart desires. Expect that you will always get what you feel you are worthy of, and you will.

I Do Not Believe in Anything

To say you do not believe in anything is not true. You know there is something grander than yourself, be it the "Universe," "God," "Love," or just "Something." Knowingness allows you to connect with your ability and to trust it truly is a gift. To strengthen your gift, you must start connecting to that knowingness, which is your spirituality, and define what that means to you. Spirituality is infinite, and there is no right way of connecting. There is just your way for you. For someone, it can be in the form of Angels. Whereas for someone else, it can be in the form of Music. Find what makes you happy and fully present in life, and follow that path to your spirituality. It will help to strengthen your openness and ability to believe.

I Am A Negative Person Since I Am Always Struggling with Negativity

You struggle with negativity even if you are an optimistic and positive person. It sounds contradictory, but it is not. Because you are sensitive to others' emotions and feelings, there is a big chance the negative ones are sticking with you for longer periods. If you do not clear yourself or someone else's energy or let something go, you will find you are being negative more often than you are positive. Removing your energy and recognizing why you find yourself in a negative space will allow you to figure out if you are truly a negative person. Chances are, you are not. You are programmed by nature to be positive, bright lights, which is why you can help so many people.

Everyone struggles with emotional imbalances. Knowing how to transform the most common imbalances will help you live a more balanced life daily.

HOW TO GROW CONFIDENCE

Our level of self-confidence may have a sizable impact on how much we love ourselves. Self-confidence can be defined as an individual's dependence on his abilities or self and his treatment of different moderation conditions without showing vanity, which keeps others away from him. At the same time does not become subservient and subject to those around him. So, the feeling of confidence can be considered a state of moderation and balance. It can be said that it is the courage to know the person himself and his self-esteem and belief in his capabilities. It necessarily reflects on others' faith and respect, so this enables him to make his decisions carefully and carefully, so he feels inner satisfaction with himself.

A self-aware person understands the strengths and weaknesses and knows how to deal with them. They also accept mistakes and realize that perfectionism is not possible. They also want to try new things. They take an example to emulate him, but lack of self-confidence is a real problem due to the person's permanent sense of inferiority, negligence, and skepticism about his ability to take responsibility or going through new experiences. In addition to the lack of ability to communicate with others and express their opinions freely, they tend to be introverted and feel depressed and worried, and do not seek to develop themselves or build new relationships. The lack of confidence may result from past conditions or problems experienced by the individual, such as dissatisfaction with personal appearance, self-esteem, and unsuccessful experiences.

How to be self-confident in front of others? Anyone can

achieve his self-confidence if they want and strive, and it may seem difficult initially, but with time this is easily achieved. For the person to appear confident in front of others, the following advice should be followed:

Always act based on having a strong and self-confident personality even with the self, which is easier to acquire over time. Trying to speak in front of others with a clear voice and understandable language without emotion, avoid anger and intense emotions. Act calmly and quench with all events, express personal opinions freely and without fear, and take the time, as this helps in selecting words and thus making the person appear more confident. Trying to use leadership qualities and firmness and displaying this in front of others without exaggeration, as the person must stand upright in front of others and not swing and vibrate in standing. Develop a plan and identify the topics and points that can talk to. Have the ability to achieve the planned objectives and share them with others, with a sense of self-respect. It is necessarily reflected in the appreciation of others' efforts—forging good relationships with others. The person can communicate visually with the other person, always initiating listening to other people's problems and providing help and advice. Training is the training of the best things that help increase the person's confidence, as a person can imagine that they explain his ideas or his research to be presented to a friend. A permanent feeling of happiness, because happiness and smile give a feeling of relaxation, and relieve our anxiety and tension in any new activity. It also helps create confidence, break the wall between people, and continuously develop oneself by learning new skills or improving past skills and overcoming weaknesses. Avoid showing weakness in front of others, avoiding hesitation and imitating other people's methods or following their decisions, while trying to create a distinct personality for the soul, and not allowing anyone to interfere in personal decisions.

What is the Right Mindset to Grow Your Confidence?

Indeed, we are often called upon to do some work that may be boring, difficult, or just displeasing. However, these may be necessary steps to achieve a goal that we have set for our professional success. How can we persuade our minds to cooperate so that we can have the confidence to do this and give our best?

Our mind is programmed to avoid anything painful and seek to do those things only to give it a pleasure. In other words, it is motivated solely by the prospect of reward for it. It is a necessary step or action that must be taken to reach our goal. If it were that easy, we would say it and do it. And on the other hand, the result's vision seems so far away that it is not a strong enough incentive to roll up our sleeves and do what needs to be done. As a result, we avoid doing this work and find all sorts of excuses such as "now is not the time," "I will do it later," etc., and we end up not taking steps forward to achieve our goal. We avoid making that phone call to the customer, writing the email, completing our presentation, etc.

So the way to entice, to fool our minds, to work together is to see this work as something individual. Remove it from the goal and add a promise of reward, as an incentive for ourselves, with its completion. For example, say to yourself, "If I dedicate myself now to completing my presentation, I will reward myself with that meal that I really like," or whatever else we consider to be a pleasure and a reward. It may seem strange, but yes! It is how the human mind works. And if we want to achieve results, to be efficient and productive, we must follow the way it works and give it what it asks of us.

Tolerance to change. Let's take the opposite side. Indecision leads to inaction. Is inaction, why do we like it? Why do we ultimately prefer it to deciding? Because we are afraid of change. Here is the self-confidence mentioned above. Like it or not, changes will happen in our lives. It is good to be the protagonist in them and not to follow them. When we are tolerant of change, it is much easier for us to make decisions confidently. Whether we lose or win the decision, we will be here to deal with it.

We can't thank everyone—one of the most important causes of indecision. We try to have everything satisfied. There is no decision without a cost; even if you don't see it, there will be. The essence of the decision is to "sacrifice" something for something else. As for the faces, it's challenging. But there we must have a beginning. Justice. The other principle is the resistance to a possible "psychological war" that some people, dissatisfied with our decision, will try to launch against us.

Those who try to please everyone, nor make decisions as "by magic" are all unhappy with them.

How to be confident? From what time we set the alarm and what breakfast we prepare until what we wear to the office and which way we choose to go to work, our lives are a series of decisions. Every day we make choices, some of no particular importance, and others that can play a decisive role in our lives.

Although we are called upon to make choices in our daily lives, making decisions is not always a simple process. Quite often, it is even more challenging to support your decisions. So how do you become more confident and supportive of the choices you make?

Decide to become more confident. The first step to becoming more confident is acknowledging that you are not very good at making choices at this time. The second step? Decide to become more confident. Stop telling yourself and those around you that you are indecisive. Think of all the little things you decided on today: the white shirt you wore, the sandwich you ordered, or the shampoo you chose. If you can make these small decisions, you can handle even the most important ones.

Don't waste time on small things. Don't waste your time dealing with trivial decisions. You don't need thirty minutes to decide what wine to choose with your food. The less time you spend on small things, the more time you will have to deal with difficult decisions.

Make a list of pros and cons. It won't take you long to record the pros and cons of a possible decision you need to make. Instead, it will make it easier for you to decide and clear your mind as to why you are making this choice. Just take a piece of paper, make two columns, and write the pros and cons. At the end of the list, you will have made your decision.

Consult your past. It is essential to learn from our mistakes so that we do not repeat them in the future. Take a look at the crucial decisions you have made so far in your life and think about the process to reach this choice. Remember the bad decisions you made. Is there anything repetitive? Insecurity; Lack of confidence; Recognize insecurities, build a relationship of trust with yourself, and make your decision wisely.

Support your decision, do your research, and get as much information as possible. Once you have collected all the data, you will be better equipped to make a well-documented decision. Now, when someone challenges your decision, you will be able to argue with them.

NLP-BASED SWISH TECHNIQUE

People possess all the resources they need; the Swish Technique is a Neuro-Linguistic Programming strategy for providing access to those resources. This easy-to-use pattern can immediately result in positive behavioral changes and improved self-esteem. Making these changes is as simple as creating a future self who has already dealt with the problem or feeling. The future self-image is superimposed on the less resourceful current image until the latter image disappears.

Exposure to the future self builds self-esteem because it improves how you think about yourself and what you can do. Because the future self has already conquered whatever problem you are dealing with, you begin to feel more confident in the moment to handle the situation. It is also true that success begets success. As you prove your future self- right by tackling problem situations formerly, your confidence and success in any difficult situation will grow.

You can use the Swish pattern for any number of problems, such as fear of public speaking, anger, low motivation, and feeling confident. You can use the pattern in virtually any situation where you want to transform current behavior. Visually speaking, the Swish pattern might look like an interior decorator's portfolio. In the first picture, you can see things as they are — a perhaps functional room but needs upgrades for its current use. In the second picture, you see the room improved and transformed. The room has been changed to accommodate current needs and functions. You are always growing and evolving. As you encounter different situations, you may need other skills to be successful in the settings. The Swish pattern can help you build those skills and discard old behaviors that no longer serve you.

Rapid Sub Modality Shifts Associate Two Mental Images

The more attractive and real the picture, the more motivation to achieve or attain the internally created state externally. Also, many values are there in creating unattractive pictures of unwanted states. Creating a dull, unattractive picture of an unwanted state makes it seem far away and unappealing compared to the positive picture. The Swish pattern is an extension of this idea.

The Swish pattern process looks much like a before and after picture. Your before-picture shows everything about what symbolizes the problem situation. For example, if you have a fear of public speaking, your before-picture might show an audience of people laughing or sleeping through your speech. You might also see yourself stumbling over words, tripping, or sweating profusely. You can even feel your heart racing as you agonize over a frozen PowerPoint presentation. In other words, you see a disaster. The Swish pattern lets you trade the before picture, the one you do not want, for an after picture, the scenario you really do want.

The after picture is entirely different. It is your idea of the presentation exactly as it could be with more feelings of confidence. Your after-picture allows you to safely create a vivid picture of yourself as someone who has already handled and overcome the problem. It is your chance to be you but improved. It does not mean you suddenly become the kind of presenter who keeps the audience laughing if that is not who you are. It does mean you bring your best authentic self — the person you are when doubt, fear, and insecurity do not hold you back.

In your after photo, the audience is pictured as attentive and engaged. You are smiling, relaxed, and confident. You feel so confident that you no longer dread public speaking; it feels natural to you.

To make your own before picture, you must first identify the trigger that initiates the undesired behavior. Use a similar chart/table to write about your feelings and triggers. Now that you have had time to consider some of your triggers choose a problem you would like to work on.

To make your own after picture, identify some of the behaviors of someone who has solved the problem you are dealing with. NLP provides a framework for modeling human excellence. Remember that if a thing has been done — in this case, managing tasks without being overcome by stress — then it can be done.

The process begins with realizing that if someone else has more success in a particular area, it does not mean they are necessarily more capable than you are. Remember the presupposition, "People are not broken." What it does mean is they use their resources differently than you do at this time. You can also change the way you use your resources to achieve the same success. Creating the after picture helps you begin to do that.

The Swish pattern can work for many problems, such as fear of public speaking or angry feelings. It can also help manage other problems, such as unwanted habits or food cravings. Remember the last time you had a food craving. The craving was probably sharp and vivid. In fact, you could almost taste the thing you craved. Maybe you could even see and smell the food or imagine how you would feel as you took your first bite. As you vividly imagined this food, the desire to consume it actually consumed you. Even if it meant blowing your diet, you knew you had to have it.

A vividly imagined feeling or experience seems almost real. This kind of powerful visualization creates strong motivation to externalize or make real the imagined experience. The Swish pattern helps eliminate unwanted behaviors and food cravings by manipulating the picture to minimize attraction and desire. In other words, say the desired food is a bowl of cookies and cream ice cream. As you think about the ice cream, you see the cookie's chunks and imagine how they will feel as you chew them. You feel the cold creaminess of the ice cream on your tongue and imagine the slight chill you feel with the first bite. The bowl feels cold in your hands, and the rich ice cream slides smoothly down your throat. The experience of eating that ice cream feels far more real than your desire to drop a pant size.

To manage a food craving, remember to turn down the unwanted visualization volume — in this case, the ice cream. Change the way you think about the ice cream, so it appears less attractive and desirable. To understand the difference, think about eating something you do not have strong feelings about. The food item is probably not sharply represented in your mind, and you do not feel as if you could almost taste it.

As you lower the volume on the unwanted picture, you must also turn up the volume on the wanted one — in this case, a smaller pant size. Go through the steps used earlier to describe a person who has already solved the problem you are dealing with. What kinds of things does a person who manages his or her ideal weight do? How does a person who maintains his or her ideal weight think? What motivates a person who keeps his or her ideal weight? Which of these attitudes and behaviors can you adopt or model to create your own excellence with weight management?

For this switch, your before-picture could show you eating the ice cream, being above your ideal weight, and holding onto self-defeating thoughts — however, you imagine that might look. The after picture shows your future self. In this picture, you are at your ideal weight and have embraced the behaviors and attitudes of someone who maintains his or her ideal weight — however, you imagine that might look. As before, hold the before picture up and quickly switch your after- picture in front of it. Let your new picture first begin to overtake and finally obscure the old one. Remember to sharpen the new picture and to make it even more attractive and compelling as you hold it in your mind's eye. Make the switch several times until your desire for the ice cream is gone.

The Swish pattern can also help you successfully eliminate unwanted behavior or build motivation to complete a dreaded task. There are no limits to how you can use the pattern. As you use the Swish Pattern to create excellence in your life, do not forget the importance of fine-tuning sub modalities.

The before picture — this is often you in a way you do not want to be regarding something you are thinking, feeling, or doing — should not be attractive or motivating. You create attraction or motivation through visualization by making the picture easy to associate with. It is more difficult to associate with or connect to a small fuzzy picture than a large, bright one.

The after picture — this is a picture of the future you are thinking, feeling, or doing something in the desired way — should be as clear and compelling as a movie. It should be easy to imagine yourself in the picture because it is so highly detailed.

This picture is created with as many of your senses as possible. It uses strong visual detail, sound, feeling, and perhaps even taste and smell. The after picture provides strong motivation to create an imagined experience.

An often-mentioned presupposition of NLP is that people have all the resources they need. In any circumstance, that leaves you feeling non-resourceful, but you have only to determine what resources you need. You can then access those resources within yourself by using the Swish pattern. The Swish pattern lets you bring the resources needed to a place where you have not used them before. It doesn't matter how long you have been experiencing with the unwanted thought or behavior pattern. When you bring additional resources to the problem situation, you change your mental map. In other words, what you see as possible expands, while what you see as impossible fades or contracts. Because you have added to your mental map, there are new distances to reach and new turns to take. Additional resources provide access to more significant territory and ultimately to the kind of success you want to create.

PERSONALITY DEVELOPMENT IS THE KEY

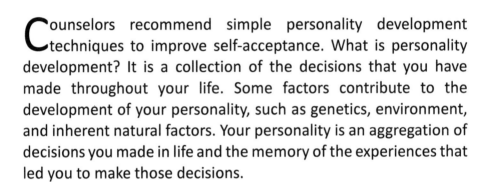

Counselors recommend simple personality development techniques to improve self-acceptance. What is personality development? It is a collection of the decisions that you have made throughout your life. Some factors contribute to the development of your personality, such as genetics, environment, and inherent natural factors. Your personality is an aggregation of decisions you made in life and the memory of the experiences that led you to make those decisions.

How Do Other People Treat You?

Self-acceptance starts during your childhood. If your parents and your siblings encouraged you and instilled in you that you are good enough, you would not have a problem accepting your adult self. Your level of acceptance is determined by how the people around you view you. Your self-acceptance will depend on what you think other people think of you. When they think highly of you, consequently you'll have a good sense of self-image. For you to build a healthy personality, your level of self-acceptance should be high.

Practice Self-Disclosure

Self-acceptance includes being able to understand your own self; you achieve this by performing simple self-disclosure exercises. Most of the time, people who have low self-esteem and self-acceptance erect walls between other people for fear of being rejected and feeling unworthy enough to be around other people.

It has to stop. If you are struggling with self-acceptance, the best thing to do is to find someone you can trust and pour your heart out, leave no stones unturned. It would help if you took out those negative thoughts from your mind. However, you must choose someone who will not judge you after you pour out everything. Choose one whom you can really trust just to hear you out, one who won't analyze or criticize, but one who will listen; hence, it would do you good if you go to a counselor instead.

Self-Awareness

After making positive progress from self-disclosure, you need to begin seeing what makes you tick. Self-disclosure is a liberating process because it lets you open up and understand the emotions and thoughts that you have might have been keeping for a very long time. Once you are aware of these negative emotions holding you, the process of ‚detachment' will be more comfortable.

Unconditionally Accepting Yourself

Self-disclosure and self-awareness prepare you for the process of self-acceptance. You have to start with honesty: be honest to yourself that you are not perfect and have flaws and weaknesses, but you have to accept yourself anyway. You have to accept that you have some good points as you have some bad points. The moment you can develop the ability to look and tell yourself honestly that you are wonderfully made even with those flaws, you have taken that bold step to unconditional self-acceptance.

Some people find it hard to admit to people of their weaknesses and flaws, so it takes a strong too many to do that. When you develop a good sense of self and accept yourself unconditionally, opening up to other people will not be so hard. Self-acceptance does not consider how people look at you.

Keep Track of Your Accomplishments

The process of self-acceptance did not end when you got the courage to face yourself in the mirror to say that you love the image that is staring back at you. There are a few things to do to ensure that you stay on course.

One useful exercise is to keep track of your good points: an inventory of your accomplishments, talents, skills, and other abilities that are uniquely yours. You must focus on these instead of your failures and mistakes. Every time you feel that you are going back to your old habit of criticizing yourself, it is best that you check back in with your inventory to remind you what you have accomplished. You have to ensure that you keep yourself motivated.

Think About the Bright Future Waiting for You

As you make improvements to yourself, you can think about how bright your future will become. Think of your potentials. Think about the unlimited possibilities of success for you. Your renewed faith in yourself gives you the courage to looktowards the future and go to wherever your future leads you. Now that you have unconditionally accepted yourself no matter what you are, you can be the person you want to become. You don't need to pretend. You can now set goals for the future and prepare and plan for them. Self-acceptance arms you with the right mindset to face all the challenges and obstacles you might encounter as you continue on with your future journey.

Use the Power of Your Mind

Don't be too hard on yourself. During this whole process of developing self-acceptance, you have to go easy on yourself. The only way you can open your mind and body to change is to accept yourself completely. While you are trying to rebuild yourself, keep in mind that it is a process, you cannot change overnight. You cannot force yourself to immediately like your

,real self.' Your mind is very powerful. Throughout the process of self-disclosure and self-awareness, up to self- acceptance, you can take advantage of the power of your mind. Beating yourself up will not benefit you at all. It is where your mind power will be needed. Practice positive affirmations every day will be helpful.

It may be true that self-acceptance starts from childhood. But there is also an aspect of your childhood that can bring in a positive effect on you: when you feel that you want to give up because you are having a hard time accepting yourself, remember that you never gave up as a toddler when you were just starting to learn how to walk. Mindpower at its best: keep in mind that what matters most is how you see yourself, and the opinion of others should never get a hold of you.

Self-talk can do you good. What you say to yourself is more important than what others say to you. Practice talking to yourself. For instance, when faced with challenges, instead of saying, ‚I can't.‘, why not say, ‚Yes, I can.‘ Replace the ‚cannot‘ to ‚can,‘ the ‚impossible‘ to ‚possible,‘ and the ‚I can't do it.‘ with ‚I can, and I will do it.‘

No matter what you feel when you wake up, face each day with many positive attitudes. When you feel good about yourself, self-acceptance comes easily. Focus on what you have instead of those things that you don't have. Be satisfied with what you have; when you can do this, you will feel comfortable, and self-acceptance is not that difficult.

Make That Big Switch

The time to act is now. Take hold of the remote control and change the channels of your life. Leave the negativity behind, and leave the self-criticisms. Love yourself more. Begin to count your blessings. Give yourself a tap on the back for a job well done.

Associate yourself with positive and confident people. When you are surrounded by people who lift you instead of criticizing you, it is easier to feel good about yourself.

Enhancing your level of self-acceptance does not necessarily mean that you will not be encountering difficulties. There is still a huge possibility that you will have to go through some challenges. Yet, when you have accepted yourself unconditionally, you will have all the confidence and the courage you need to get past those obstacles and challenges. Remember that it is not essential to get things done the right way; what matters is you keep ongoing.

SELF-ACCEPTANCE AND FEELINGS OF INFERIORITY

A fair division of the population struggles with the results of comparing themselves to others and trying to achieve "perfection" and from low self-esteem or self-confidence. Unfortunately, distorted body image and social media issues are common problems, but they are not the only areas with which people struggle. Whatever the struggle may be, a standard set of tools can be used to overcome a negative self- image and false beliefs. An individual must refocus, unearth the falsities behind the expectations, and move toward self- acceptance. The definition of self-acceptance is reasonably straightforward - accepting who you truly are, with all your strengths and your imperfections. It's a simple enough concept, but it takes time, practice, and patience.

Take, for instance, Layla's story:

"It was not until I was in my forties that I had an epiphany that I could not recall a single time in my life where I felt like I belonged – that I was good enough. What a sad way to live life.

Looking back, I do not know when these feelings began. I just know that they have always existed. In Elementary School, these feelings manifested in fears of "not fitting in" and that no one liked me. I felt like an outsider in every way, from the clothes I wore to how I interacted with others. I did not just feel this way around my peers, but also around adults. These feelings were not limited to school either. I also felt this way

at church, where I should have felt very safe and very accepted.

By all accounts, I should have been a pleased child. I was a straight-A student, my teachers adored me, and I won contests and awards. In fifth grade, I was even crowned queen at the annual school beauty pageant. I should have been so happy, but I recall spending so many sad, sad days. I remember sitting in my front yard, feeling so lost and just want to disappear.

As I was working through my new epiphany and believing that I was making progress, I was at an outdoor concert one evening and needed to use the restroom. Walking through the crowd, I was suddenly overwhelmed by that all too familiar feeling that I should not be here and that everyone who looked my direction could see that I was inferior to them.

Many of my battles with self – most of my struggles with self– stem from my body image issues. "Being fat" seems as if it has always been an issue for me. I can pinpoint the beginning of that battle to about seventh or eighth grade when I suddenly gained a lot of weight. My parents put me on a diet. I recall taking my lunch of tuna, lettuce, and pineapple to lunch every day. I did lose the weight by my Freshman year in High School, but it has been a struggle ever since."

From where do such feelings of inferiority stem? Many professionals theorize that our acceptance of self is based on how accepted we felt by our parents. If our parents sent us negative messages about who we were and what we could accomplish, they followed us as we began to develop our concept of self.

For some, self-worth feelings are directly connected to performance and achievement because their parents transmitted a message that value is connected to behavior.

Parents often do this inadvertently and do not see that they are focusing more on negative behaviors than on positives. The child then begins to identify themselves and their worth with the negative behaviors – their failures.

In some cases, the parent's efforts to curb negative behavior, or what they perceive to be negative behavior, goes much further than a lack of positive parenting.

For example, an overcritical father may be so frustrated with a child's inability to do well in academics that the child internalizes beliefs that he is stupid. A mother's efforts to help an overweight child lose weight may result in developing body image issues that follow her into adulthood.

Of course, there are cases of child maltreatment in which physical, sexual, or emotional abuse can result in negative consequences throughout the survivor's life. Many mental health professionals hold that, at the very least, most individuals learn from their parents that they are only conditionally acceptable. Therefore, if you don't live up to whatever arbitrary standards you have created in your mind, you are a failure.

While they will not recognize the damage occurring to their psyche, most children will realize that they do not like feeling unfairly punished, criticized, or hurt by their parents.

Ironically, however, they end up committing these same ills on themselves, as adults.

You may have heard it said that as we age, we turn into our parents. It is very true in the way that we treat ourselves. We internalize negative childhood feelings of angst, powerlessness, and worthlessness until our ability to love ourselves is compromised appropriately. Our vision of self can also be scarred by pivotal moments when we experienced something so life-altering that it follows us throughout our life. For some, this might be bullying. For others, it might be an embarrassing incident at school. A statement made by a peer or adult authority-figure that exposes a perceived flaw can do almost irreparable damage in some. We then, unknowingly, punish ourselves in several ways.

Some people will try to compensate for feeling unworthy by undertaking self-improvement projects. Bookshelves, magazine racks, television programming, and the internet are overflowing with materials on self-improvement, a testament to the fact that our society members feel like they are not good enough and need always to be trying harder and doing better. Others will avoid taking risks out of fear of failure. Still, others live in the past or worry about the future, continually reliving past failures or in anxiety over what trouble may lie ahead.

Living like this is a survival mechanism for the individual, a protective wall that insulates them from feeling out of control. If they always expect the worst, then when failure comes, it is no surprise, and they can say, "I told you so!" The individual does not realize that they are robbed of the joy of living in the present moment. Always staying busy is another way that some people try to cope with feelings of inadequacy. Keep busy! Do more. Achieve more. Set goals!

Unfortunately, in an attempt to make themselves feel better, some begin to look for and focus on other people's faults. Biologically speaking, the more times these types of thoughts are processed, the more the neural pathways become ingrained. They become like a well-worn, familiar old pathway that we can take without much thought and practically blindfolded.

We have identified the problem and talked about possible reasons for lack of self-acceptance, but how does one overcome and learn to accept themselves wholly and lovingly? Experts disagree on a specific methodology, but we must have the correct tools and practice.

Lessons can be learned from religions, spiritual practices, secular therapeutic practices, and anecdotal evidence from those who have succeeded in learning to love and accept themselves.

SELF-AWARENESS

Before we begin talking about the origins of self-awareness, we should define what we're talking about. The self-awareness we're talking about here is defined as having a clear understanding of your personality, both your strengths plus weaknesses as well as your thoughts, beliefs, emotions, and motivations. Being acutely self-aware means, in short, you know yourself, and you understand your motivations. It often requires taking a "deep dive" into what has shaped you and how that interacts with your emotions and thoughts to guide your behavior. It also means checking in with yourself at any moment to understand how events are impacting your emotional state. And self-awareness is the foundation for emotional intelligence as well as self-leadership and mature adulthood. But where does this originate, and how do we develop it?

The Origin of Self-Awareness

Understanding self-awareness means understanding a little bit about the brain. There are three basic systems in the brain:

- the neocortex, which is our conscious mind where most of our thoughts happen

- the limbic system, which is the subconscious "heart-centered" area where our emotions arise

- the basal ganglia, which is the unconscious "gut-centered" area where our instincts are activated

All three areas are involved in cultivating self-awareness. The neocortex is our conscious mind that we can access at any time.

The limbic system is our subconscious mind, where we store emotions, value judgments, and memories. Lastly, the basal ganglia use the information it receives from our gut to generate an unconscious instinctual response. It does so without checking with the other two regions of the brain (Cascio 2015; Strecher 2015). You can begin to see how all of these regions can affect our feelings and our experience at any moment in time.

As we go through life accumulating experiences, we react to those experiences using all three systems. We respond with our conscious neocortex--that is, we think about and rationalize the experience--and we use the subconscious limbic system to generate and store emotions we have around the experience. Those emotions create a gut feeling that goes through the basal ganglia to activate appropriate instinctual responses. So, for example, if you feel fear, you may be analyzing what to do, but your negative emotions are being recorded and stored, and your gut feeling is stimulating an instinctual fear response. Most of this is happening on a subconscious or unconscious level. To generate self- awareness, we want to consciously access all of these areas to fully understand what we think and feel and guide our actions.

As with learning any new skill, cultivating self-awareness means passing through four stages (Jeffrey 2019):

- Unconscious incompetence--this is where you don't know how bad you are at something until you try. You don't know you can't play the piano until you play a few chords.

- Conscious incompetence--this is where you are now aware of the fact that you are not good at doing something. You now understand that you can't play the piano.

- Conscious competence--this is where you make a committed effort to learn a new skill, and because of your dedication and practice, you have now reached a level where you are reasonably good at this skill. You can play the piano. But, for this stage, you have to be willing to work through some uncomfortable feelings that arise due to your conscious incompetence.

- Unconscious competence--this is the brass ring. It is where you can now perform the skill effortlessly. You can sit down at the piano without sheet music and play songs easily. It is the part where the magic happens.

Most people will give up when those uncomfortable feelings arise — as with any skill, developing self-awareness means passing through these stages.

Why We Lack Self-Awareness

As with any skill, cultivating self-awareness demands practice and dedication. It's uncomfortable to feel incompetent, and so, most people will give up at that stage of the process. Many people fail to develop self-awareness because, although they try, they target only the conscious neocortex rather than all three systems. A conscious connection to all three systems is a must if we truly understand the root of our thoughts, feelings, and actions. Suppose we increase our sensitivity to our emotions and instincts. In that case, we can more thoroughly explore our thoughts, beliefs, and biases, and it is only then that we can truly understand our behavior. Another problem in developing true self-awareness is that most people think they're self-aware, but very few are.

According to a multi-year study by The Eurich Group, a group of psychologists who provide executive coaching and leadership development programs for businesses, only 10 to 15 percent of people actually exhibit the characteristics of self- awareness; this even though some 85 to 90 percent of people think they are self-aware (Eurich 2018). Real self-awareness means being able to identify your values, goals, flaws, and your motivations, all with an understanding of how your past has influenced your behavior. It means acting consciously in every area of your life, exploring emotions as they arise, digging to get at the reasons for your triggers, and acting with intentionality to not only preserve but grow your self- awareness. It means understanding your place in the universe and the impact your actions have on yourself and others. Developing this takes a lot of work, and many people have too much fear of those uncomfortable emotions and instinctive reactions that will undoubtedly happen along the way. That's why we lack self-awareness, but if you've realized that you're among the 85 - 90 percent of those who have not developed their self-awareness, what can you do to cultivate it?

Gaining Self-Awareness Through Others

While there are many things that other people cannot do for you as you develop your self-awareness, one thing that they can do is help you understand some of your own strengths and weaknesses through effective feedback. Effective feedback does not mean criticism. Instead, it is honest and kind, specific, not general, descriptive, not critical; and focused on helping you build your strengths rather than highlight your weaknesses. Having a life coach or even a trusted friend who can give you this kind of feedback can help you understand areas of your behavior that you might not even realize are affecting your life. It is often easier to see shortcomings in other people than it is to see them in yourself. It isn't necessarily because you're critical of other people, but because you can see how your good friends limit themselves or even sabotage their own success.

In contrast, they are too close to the situation. Likewise, you can be too close to your situation to understand how others see you. That's how others can help us see things we might not be willing to look at without their help. Life coaches are trained to help you with this kind of thing, but if you don't have one of those, you can ask a good friend to provide you with some effective feedback.

MINDFUL SELF –COMPASSION

Mindfulness helps you build self-love. Before we delve into how it helps you build self-love, let us understand mindfulness. Mindfulness is the act of being present in every moment, concentrating on what you are doing at any point in time, and refusing to dwell on past mistakes and future worries.

How Mindfulness Helps You Build Self- Love

When you engage in mindful practices such as mindful breathing, meditation, yoga, etc., you focus your mind on the things you have been overlooking all your life. Mindfulness makes you more grateful for the things and abilities you have.

Mindfulness also enables you to take note of things that add value to your life. Things you have always considered insignificant such as your ability to talk people into changing certain habits, your ability to make people smile amidst worries, and your ability to come up with solutions to difficult puzzles, etc. Mindfulness also helps you notice all the things you have going for you and enables you to love and respect who you are. How can you practice mindfulness to develop self-respect and improve self-love? Here are some ideas to guide you:

Know What You Think, Feel, And Want Most Times

Mindful people keep track of their most dominant thoughts, feelings, and desires. When you become more mindful of your thoughts and feelings, it becomes easier to control your flow of thoughts and emotions.

Separate Your Positive Thoughts and Feelings from The Negative Ones

Once you become mindful of your most dominant thoughts and feelings, you will be in a position to sieve your thoughts and separate the healthy from the unhealthy ones. Imagine a deep hole beneath the surface of the earth where you can channel all thoughts that make building self-love challenging. Retain all positive thoughts and willingly replay them in your mind. You can make positive thoughts into some affirmations and repeat them as often as possible until they become a part of you.

Train Yourself to Become More Mindful of What Goes on Around You

Making mindfulness a part of your daily life will increase self-love and the quality of life you live. Let us learn how you can make mindfulness a part of your daily life:

Practice Mindful Breathing

Mindful breathing is an aspect of mindfulness that helps you concentrate on how your breath cycles come and go. Mindful breathing begins with locating a suitable quiet spot free from any distractions. Anywhere around your home or office should be ideally provided; the place is serene, secluded and conducive to helping you easily master the art of concentration.

Once you find a location, settle into your most comfortable posture, and concentrate on your breathing, taking in the whole whoosh sound as the air rushes in and out of your windpipe, the time it takes you to complete a cycle of breath, and how many breaths you can take in a minute. Do not think about anything else; only your breath matters at this point.

Develop A Mantra

A mantra is simply a word or sound you repeat to help you

focus and concentrate during mindful exercises. Your mantra can be a word, a phrase, a sentence, or just a sound. Developing and focusing on a mantra during your mindful exercises can help you become grounded/centered enough to notice the most lovable and amazing things about yourself and life in general.

Your mantra can be one of the positive thoughts you created into an affirmation or any other thing you consider positive and motivating enough to make you love yourself more. It can be a thought centered on your major strengths and talents. This mantra should form your focus as soon as you become accustomed to your breath and its pattern. Your mantra can be something like, "I'm the best singer, athlete, student, employee, best singer, actor, or investor."

Be Mindful of Everything Else

The state of mindfulness should not stop at your breathing and mantra; you should be able to transfer it to every other activity you engage in during the day. These activities should include the ones you engage in at home and those you engage in when you are at the office or school. When you take note of what goes on around you during the day and how you handle issues that crop up in your line of work, the respect you have for yourself will grow, and naturally, your self-esteem will start on a bullish run.

Practice Self-Respect

Practicing self-respect is one of the most important aspects of practicing self-love. If you cannot respect yourself, it will be impossible to love yourself for who you are. You must find something to respect about yourself before you can find something to love about yourself. How can you practice self-respect? Here are some tips:

Carry Yourself with Dignity

The way you carry yourself tells a lot about how much you

respect yourself and influences how people respect you. Take a cue from charismatic people and the way they carry themselves. You can start by always walking briskly with your head held high and your shoulders squared. Even while seated, sit like someone sure of himself/herself by sitting straight with your legs stretched in front of you, hands clasped, and on your lap.

Present Yourself in The Most Respectable Way

There is a direct link on how you present yourself and how people address you. A great deal of how you present yourself has to do with what you wear and how you wear it. One school of thought says others address you depending on how you dress. It is something to consider maybe.

Have A High Opinion of Yourself

You do not need all the money, fame, or success in the world before you start seeing the royalty in you. Always treat yourself as if you have already attained the heights you are aiming for in life. Imagine the future you are working towards and see yourself there. It will increase your self-respect and self-love.

VALUES

Your values are a massive part of who you are. They dictate what you feel is OK in life, from you and others. They are principles that mean a lot to you, that you uphold to your greatest ability. They offer a great benefit to you and are something you revere highly.

Most people hold onto their values religiously, refusing to differ on them. Those with low self-esteem may be more inclined to give up on their values or "let them slide" when a pushy person encourages it, however, because they don't believe their values are worth standing up for. It is not an ethical weakness as much as a refusal to believe in yourself and take care of yourself as you see fit. You allow others to run your life, which robs you of the power you were born with and rightfully should practice.

It is where saying "no" comes in. Saying no is one of the essential skills you can gain in life. The power to say no often eludes those with low self-esteem. But you deserve to have your boundaries respected, and the only way to win that respect is by telling people no. People don't know what the rules are; they will still test the rules if they do. Telling people no might make them mad, but more often than not, it merely encourages them to respect you. A marked difference will appear in your life if you start to adhere to your values and tell people to respect your boundaries.

Recognizing Your Values

Things that make you well up with passion make the heart pump that evokes an immediate and strong response from you –

these things are your values. When someone humiliates you, he has somehow violated your values. Investigating what makes you heated points you to what your values are. Start to outline your values in a journal to get a more lucid picture of who you are and what you should stand up for.

You may consider looking at the sample value list below to understand better what you stand for. Consider your political party, religion, raising, and how you raise your own children if you have any also to get more ideas. Think of what you try to bring to your job and what you expect of others. Also, hearken back to when you were happiest and what you did to reach that state of ecstasy.

A Sample List of Values

In case you are still unclear on what values can include, here is a sample list.

Your values may have to do with religion, in which case they are equally valid to commonly shared cultural and personal ideals that others have. Prohibit others that make you feel guilty or "weird" for being religious. Your values still matter and should be honored. If you follow a religion, think of how important it is to you and what rules it mandates for you to follow, such as treating your body like a temple or turning the other cheek.

Your values may have to do with how you were raised. Perhaps you were raised to be a lady or gentleman, and you hate it when people don't say thank you when you hold the door open or pull out a chair for them. Your manners are things that you hold dear from childhood. You may also be a feminist, or you may not be.

Political values depend on who you are as a person. It is not uncommon for a child to grow up in a conservative household and become a liberal, or vice versa. Your political values may not depend on your rearing but rather on the humanitarian values you hold dear to your heart. Your political party affiliation sheds light upon the values you hold dear in society.

Your values also likely have to do with ethics. Most people have a basic idea of right and wrong. These ethics are rooted in our culture. The most basic include defending free speech, looking presentable, being professional, keeping your business to yourself, not gossiping, and never committing sins like adultery, theft, and murder. While these values have religious roots, they are ultimately common American values that most Americans share. These values can shift slightly if you are from another country.

Some other values many people hold are:

- Spending time with family
- Raising children with love and support.
- Having free time
- Treat pets like family.
- Animal rights
- Being creative
- Beauty
- Accomplishment
- Taking the necessary risks
- Nourishing healthy friendship
- Love and dating
- Cooperating with others
- Having compassion
- Forgiving others
- Contributing what you can to any worthy project or charity
- Learning what you can
- Being enthusiastic
- Being polite and friendly
- Smiling

- Being kind to others
- Treating others with respect
- Being loyal to your loved ones and causes
- Making money
- Working hard
- Doing a job well the first time.
- Having peace on first
- Leaving a clean Earth for our children
- Reaping maximum profit
- Achieving happiness
- Taking care of your body
- Winning
- Being the best, you can be

How to Prioritize Your Values

Values set your personal priorities and help you reach decisions. Therefore, they are always of the utmost importance. No one can tell you that your values are wrong or that you should change them. People will certainly try to tell you this and push you to abandon your values in favor of theirs, but they are not right. Adhering to your personal set of values without budging is the true meaning behind "prioritizing your values." Make your values come first, and the opinions of others last.

Life is at its fullest when you are living according to your values. You don't feel so good when you do things in your job or life that you sense are wrong or when you disagree with your own actions. When you let people stress you into doing things that go against your values, you feel spineless and sick to your stomach. Standing up for your values and matching your actions to your beliefs allows you to live a balanced, aligned life that you can be proud of. It helps your self-esteem swell up like a balloon, fueled by the helium of personal strength and pride.

Getting to know your values is the first and foremost way to discover how to live your life best. If your job, studies, or other pursuits clash with your values, you need to reevaluate what you are doing in life. If your partner, family, or friends push you to continually ignore your values in favor of theirs, reconsider your relationships. People who love you will never ask you always to do things that you feel opposed to.

When you learn what your values are, you can listen to your heart. You will feel queasy and terrible if you violate your own scruples. Learn to say no when you are asked to do things that make you feel that sickness in the pit of your gut. Tell people what your personal rules are and set consequences for when people break said rules. It is OK to end relationships with those who refuse to acknowledge and accept your boundaries. It is also OK to quit a job that repeatedly asks you to do things that don't rub well with your personal sense of ethics. Bullies and abusers will often try to twist your mind around and tell you that your values are wrong so that they can have their way with you, but when you learn to put your values first above all else, you learn to stand up to these people and no longer take their abuse.

Value prioritization also helps you make decisions when they are most difficult. Of course, life sometimes forces us to make gut-wrenching sacrifices or uncomfortable compromises. List your top ten values and then determine their ranking, from the most important to ten being the least important. The first value may be family and the second is the family pet. You may find that paying your dog's huge vet bill is not as important as feeding your child based on this value ranking, so that helps you make a tough and painful decision. It is not a fun decision, but it is one that suits best with your values.

Finally, prioritizing your values can help you evaluate people in your life and new people entering it as you begin creating a successful environment and taking the trash out. Watch how people respond to your values and how they respect them. Watch if a person attempts to dissuade you from your own values, humiliates you over them, or refuse to respect them. Any person who blatantly disrespects your values is crummy indeed. He will confidently destroy your self-esteem and your sense of self to get what he wants, and then once he is finished using you, he will flounce away, unscathed and satiated, in search of his future victim.

Don't be weak – you deserve better. Filter out the disrespectful people and only entertain those who can uphold your values. It doesn't mean that someone needs to share all of your values – just that they need to treat you as a human being and not walk all over you. Generally, however, people find comfort in those who are most similar to themselves. You will most likely not get along well with someone who does not share your values and does many things you disagree with.

Finding your values is an amazing and enlightening part of getting to know yourself, a journey that helps you fall in love with who you really are. But as time wears on, your strong sense of values may begin to soften and fade. It is why reaffirming your values every six months or so is a highly recommended part of this journey. Write your top ten values down in a visually appealing way and save the document on your computer or in a treasure chest or some other safe, personal place. Pull them out and review them twice a year.

On the other hand, you can display them prominently in a place where you will often see them so that you are reminded of them each day. It is only a good idea if you don't mind others seeing your values, which you shouldn't because you have nothing to be ashamed of. Your values are just as important as the other guys, and they are not wrong, no matter what anyone tries to tell you.

DECLUTTERING EVERY ASPECT OF LIFE

Decluttering' is a term being used in various ways, such as reducing relationships, distractions, and cleaning. Initially, the term was coined for a minimalist lifestyle where people are looking to see fewer items around the home that collect dust and cause anxiety. We have taken the term and applied it to more areas of our lives to gain more happiness in life, work, and relationships. It is a concept that will help boost confidence and increase self-motivation.

Physical Clutter

Physical clutter refers to materialistic concepts. Look around the room you are in; what do you see? As you observe the room, are there things you have not looked at for six months? Are there things you put on a table for convenience rather than necessity? As an example, let's say our busy person who cannot take cybersecurity courses lives in a small space. Due to the life business, the mail is on multiple surfaces, journals are everywhere, books are stacked all over the place, and dust bunnies are additional companions to the pets.

How do you think the person might feel coming into the home, going to the workspace, and seeing things everywhere, with no clear organization, pattern, or empty surface? Each person is different, but it is more apt to say the person would find it difficult to classify. The clutter pushes the anxiety to increase, so the person starts thinking about all the tasks that need to be completed, the family drama that takes time and money away from other goals, and now the motivation to get work done is at an all-time low. The person wants to tackle all goals, but the pressure and anxiety to do the most important work first, what makes money, increases. This increase in pressure and anxiety reduces the motivation; the person wants to seek something to make them happy or at least feel less tired and believe the brain can ensure the completion of the most important goal.

If the person instead took ten minutes a day to put things in their place, eliminate the useless mail, and organize items used daily, the workspace would be clear, decluttered, and useable. The motivation would be there to complete the task without anxiety increasing. The focus would be on the important goal and not on everything else that needs to be done but is not met.

From the example, you can see the cyclical problems that physical clutter could create, depending on your personality. Some people can live in a mess and never see it. It could create more anxiety to reduce the clutter than to leave it.

What type of person are you? If you believe you can deal with physical clutter yet never seem to be motivated, it is time to change.

Some people can leave clutter, ignoring the mess, because their laser focus is on one goal, but the key is the person has the motivation to complete the work and is doing so, regardless of the world around them. Few can be done to ignore or to reduce the clutter.

Ignore the Clutter for Motivation

Let's say you are the first example, where the clutter is bothering you, but you do not have time to fix it because the goal is too important. You do not want to lose to yourself and wish to gain motivation.

- Create a tunnel vision. If you have a shirt with a hood, wear it and put the hood up, blocking your peripheral vision.
- Move things closer that you will need while completing the

task, such as a glass of water close and within your vision for easy reach.

- If you are using a computer, but time is increasing anxiety, hide the clock.

- Turn on relaxing music, if possible, such as new age or classical—something that instills a relaxed mind, and not something that will cause your heart to race.

- Focus only on what is in front of you that matters to complete the task.

- When you have completed a quarter of the task, stand up, remove something from the work area that creates clutter. Put it elsewhere, place it where it belongs, or throw the trash away.

- Go back to your task with your tunnel vision.

Keep to these steps until the task is complete. Set small goals to meet during the significant task. For instance, if you know a task should take you five hours, and you will need lunch in the middle of it, set a goal to meet before the meal, and reward yourself with lunch.

Let's say you need to type up a report that is 10,000 words, and you can type 2,000 words in an hour. By noon, you should have 5,000 words complete, and thus you have half of the report for after your meal.

You gained a break, food to keep you going, and you completed a goal, which can help reduce the anxiety of meeting the deadline by the end of the day.

In such a scenario, you may set sixty seconds aside each hour to stand up, stretch, and sit back down to help keep your body active. Studies show if you have been sitting, you need to stand to help bring back energy.

Reduce the Clutter

You have one tactic for dealing with physical clutter that may be impacting your motivation and anxiety. Let's consider a different option. You may discover that you cannot focus on the important task until you reduce the clutter. Yes, you may want to attack the entire problem, but for now, to reduce the clutter in your work area is imperative.

- Clean up your work surface.

- Start with the mail, throw away the envelopes, and put the bills or paperwork in an area meant for such things. You might put everything in the respective folders or a stack on the corner of your desk.

- Work through the areas that are bothering you, such as putting books near the shelves where they go.

- Once the surface is clean, and your vision sees cleanliness, wipe the surface of dirt, debris, or pet hair.

- Now, you have accomplished a goal.

- Use this completion and the feelings it provided to begin the imperative task.

You gain more focus in this method than you might with tunnel vision, which ultimately saves you time. If you consistently see the mess and cannot ignore it, your thoughts are on the clutter, which means you reduce your focus on the goal and ensure it takes you longer—possibly past deadline— to meet the goal.

Decide what type of personality you have regarding tunnel vision or clutter reduction. Use the ways that suit you best to work on decluttering your physical surface.

The key factor is to realize that small goals throughout the process will provide you with a sense of accomplishment and happiness, which will increase your overall motivation.

The simple act of starting and completing a simple task makes you want to see what else you can do. It is the dopamine that ensures your desire to stay on task is there.

The example is more about a work situation, where physical clutter creates distractions and anxiety. You may have a life that allows you plenty of time to perform daily routines, such as cleaning, but you continuously avoid it because there is nothing to push you.

Eliminating Clutter When Motivation Is A Factor

You are a person with plenty of time, and you think to yourself, ‚Oh, I'll do that tomorrow.‘ Then you find something to distract you. Perhaps, your emotional state is precarious due to life struggles leading to anxiety and depression; therefore, you ask what the point of doing anything is. For anxiety and depression, seeking help is necessary. When you are distracted by fun and entertainment rather than timing issues or emotional stress, the following tips might help.

- Set a goal, such as ten minutes spent on decluttering and cleaning.
- Turn on music, the TV you know you can listen to in the background, or ask someone to time you.
- Being the task.

Studies show that you will want to finish the task once you start something, even with a time goal in mind. Now, understand it will not work for everyone. A person with ADHD can create a goal and leave it unfulfilled by getting distracted about something else.

You must understand your personality before you can follow tips that work for you.

It is even better when you understand you had set a time limit and completed the task before the limit occurred. For example, a person might have set a goal of reaching half the word count by noon and discovered they did more than that; they exceeded it by 100 words before 11:55 am.

The point is you need to understand who you are, your strengths and limitations, and the rewards that will make you smile. Once you have those ingredients, you will start creating new pathways to ensure motivation helps you complete any task you set your mind to, and thus you will take on opportunities that become available.

Emotional Clutter

Reducing physical clutter is often easier than dealing with emotional baggage when it comes to getting motivated. But there are things you can do to help alleviate some of your concerns to help bring back your motivation.

Eliminate any possible diseases, illnesses, or disorders that could affect your motivation. Depression keeps being mentioned because it does have an enormous impact on your ability to complete tasks. Depression is linked with hormonal imbalances to be related to diseases or disorders like hyper or hypothyroid. Other hormones, if not supplied enough, can mimic depression. Depression is one medical and mental condition that can be addressed with medication.

Anxiety is another psychological issue that can relate to illness, as much as it relates to one's mental health. Fear may be a constant companion or situational. It is possible you can take medication for the anxiety if it is a constant companion. There are other methods such as meditation and breathing techniques you can use to reduce anxiety while it is at its height.

When it comes to emotional clutter, the best thing to do is to address things head-on. Do not let them build up and become more problematic. Working through the things that affect you the most is imperative. But, not always possible. For example, a person could have so many things going on from too much work, too little money, housing concerns, child care concerns, and quite a bit else than focusing on the essential task because difficult. Instead of putting aside the things that are not as imperative, you might continue to think of everything all at once and feel like your mind is going to explode.

GETTING OUT OF YOUR COMFORT ZONE

All of us have a desire to step out of our comfort zone at some point. We see other people doing exciting things, and we internally want to be a part of something new and thrilling. But even though that desire exists, something gets in our way, and we find ourselves paralyzed in the cocoon of comfort we've made. There is a purpose why it is so difficult to break free from our comfort zone, and with a little understanding of what it is, you can make a few simple adjustments that will allow you to do so.

What is Your Comfort Zone?

Your comfort zone is a behavioral dynamic where your routines and habits all fit together nicely. It is the safe place you go to where there is a minimal risk (or at least risk that is manageable) and, by extension, less stress. When you are in your comfort zone, you are mentally secure, content, with low anxiety and stress.

While staying in your comfort zone lowers your level of stress, and it gives you a 'safe haven' from the unknown world around you, it has its own limitations. As long as you remain in that low-stress environment, you cannot progress or grow.

Our stress levels have to be slightly higher than what we experience when we are comfortable to improve at anything. If we stay in that place for too long, we cannot progress.

It is true; your comfort zone can be a good thing. It is a safe-place where you can go mentally and emotionally. Leaving it means taking on a whole new set of risks and venturing into unchartered territory, which could turn out to be either positive, or it could be negative. But there is a good reason to try to break out of that safe spot and seek out new things.

What You're Missing Out On

Pushing to the point where you can grow is the only place where you can improve your performance in anything you do. It enhances your productivity and gives you a lot more skills you'll be able to rely on. Think about some of these benefits when it comes to stepping out of your comfort zone.

Increased Productivity: No one enjoys the pressure that comes with deadlines and expectations placed on us. If we remain in our safe-place, we do the minimum required for us to get by. Without the internal drive to do more and learn new things, we fall into a pattern of appearing busy but leaving our minds free to wander wherever they may go. But, if you push beyond that flat-line, you'll be able to find smarter ways to work and get more done at the same time.

Adapt Better to Changes: Regularly stepping out of our comfort zone, pushing the boundaries teaches you how to adapt to changes better. If you regularly push the limits, taking risks in a controlled manner, challenging yourself in various new environments, you learn to adjust to things that make you uncomfortable. As a result, you widen your comfort zone, allowing you to incorporate more into your daily life.

It'll Get Easier: After you've pushed the boundaries a few times, it won't be so frightening or challenging to do. Regularly opening up to new ideas can teach us new things, allow us to see the world in a whole new way, and inspire us to expand even more. Each time we do, we learn to view the world in a different light, and we are more motivated to expend our energy in wildly rewarding ways.

There are many benefits to widening our comfort zone that can linger far longer than the initial fear you might have experienced in the beginning. The advancements you'll gain through new skills and experiences will far outweigh the negatives you might be worried about.

Think about all the things you are afraid of, whether speaking in public or traveling to a new country. Most of it comes from worry about what you think will happen. It's all in the future, and your mind is playing various scenarios about the possibilities. You are allowing your mind to create false expectations.

Let's take speaking in public, for example. Most people have that fear of speaking out in public. What is on your mind when you have to speak in front of people. You automatically think, 'they won't like me,' 'I'll forget what I have to say,' 'I'll mess up' or 'They'll boo me.' We all think of that, or we think of something similar. But, in reality, those kinds of things never really happen. Our minds have just convinced us that we are not worthy of respect, appreciation, reward, or whatever. As a result, our minds will create the worst possible scenario in any given situation.

Since we cannot predict the future, and the odds of those things happening are very limited, our minds have created these false expectations and delivered them to us as fact, therefore paralyzing us to the point that we cannot act. It doesn't mean that you have to push the boundaries all the time. There is no bad thing with being comfortable, but if we get too comfortable and never challenge ourselves, our comfort zone will stagnate, and our world and the things in it will shrink. We need to push the limits sometimes to grow.

Training Your Mind to be Brave

By following some basic strategies, you can start small and build upon your successes until you reach the point where you are brave enough to venture boldly into new territory. You might want to play it close to the vest at first, but as you progress, you'll find that stretching the limits can bring out the best in you.

Do routine things a little differently: This initial step allows you to stay within your comfort zone without experiencing something completely new. If you drive to work every day, rather than take the same route, try a new one.

Chances are you are very familiar with the different roads in your community so that you won't be driving in unfamiliar territory. You're only changing the time you are on that particular road. It puts familiar things in a different light. After you have successfully changed some of your routine habits this way, you'll start to feel a little more confident in your ability to do something different.

Slow down: When we are in our comfort zone, we live mostly on automatic pilot, and we can whisk through tasks without even realizing we're doing them. Learning to slow down on unfamiliar tasks can quickly make you uncomfortable. Take the time to do things at a slower pace, taking note of your actions. As you do, observe your task as an outsider and then try to intervene and develop different, more efficient ways to improve them. Mentally defend your reasons for doing things the way you do. It might be enough to give you a little nudge to make some changes in your life.

Make a snap decision: Now and then, decide without thinking. When we have to step out of our comfort zone, we tend to overthink things and often dedicate a lot of time to finding reasons not to do something. It doesn't have to be a vital decision, so start by considering something small. If you eat at the same place every day, consider trying a new place. If you eat the same foods all the time, try something new. It will give your learning curve a kickstart and teach you that you can fully trust your inner judgment.

Make small, incremental steps: In the beginning, it will be difficult to make even the smallest step, but if you can muster up the courage to take those tiny baby steps, you will still get the same benefits as you would the bigger ones. Whether you jump into the water with both feet or you start by sticking one toe in, you're going to get wet just the same. Don't push too far, and you might be surprised at where you end up, one little tiny baby step at a time.

And you know what you gain from doing new things? More self-confidence, which naturally leads to better self-discipline.

HOW TO BUILD SOLID SELF-ESTEEM

Self-esteem can be defined as the image a person has of himself. It is an essential factor in determining the kinds of experiences an individual will have in life and their emotional reactions. A person with low self-esteem tends to feel useless and uncared for a while, readily blaming himself and thinking that suffering is his or her due. He or she is the one who is actually the source of his own anguish by choosing to listen to his inner critic and wallowing in depressive and negative emotional states. To get out of this vicious cycle of self-abuse, there are various means to help a person build his self-worth.

First, an individual plagued with low self-esteem must acknowledge that he is suffering from this issue. Secondly, he or she should write down his or her perceived strengths and weaknesses. Thirdly, he or she will need to think up situations where they have displayed such qualities and shortcomings, and then analyze his emotional states and behaviors in the respective occurrences. For example, a person who has made a mistake at work will condemn himself/herself for failing at his tasks and thus undergo negative emotional reactions like guilt, worthlessness, and depression. After going through the exercise of introspection, the individual should then imagine him or herself to be a highly self-assured person or picture a self-confident colleague and reflect on how his alter self or the other person would have reacted in similar situations. Finally, they should seek help from their closest friends and family by asking them how they perceive him and what they see as his strengths and flaws. It will enable him to recognize how he or she perceives him or herself if not in tune with reality and how others perceive him or her.

Moreover, the person with low self-esteem should learn to silence their inner critic and replace that voice with that of an inner motivational coach. He or she needs to develop confidence by voicing his opinions in situations where he can contribute positively. The individual can also try new experiences regularly to boost his self-image, such as learning to play a new instrument, decorating cakes, volunteering with a charity, or joining a local sports team. Furthermore, overcoming his fears will also help increase his sense of self- achievement and self-worth. For example, a person who is afraid to tread in deep waters may persuade himself to conquer his fear and swim beyond the shallow end of the pool. New adventures and experiences will enable the person to test their limits and build their self-esteem by successfully overcoming personal mental barriers, which hindered him/her from leading a positive life.

Control Your Emotion.

Emotional Intelligence is an essential aspect in determining the way a person lives his life. It defines the level of self-confidence a person possesses, which will enable him to tackle day-to-day problems. According to Daniel Goleman's Five Pillars of Emotional Intelligence, self-awareness is a prerequisite to having high self-esteem. It consists of being aware of your emotional states and the effects they have on other people. A person should be able to identify, analyze, and understand his own emotions and impulses. How a person reacts to a particular situation depends on his emotional awareness and ability to control it. Another piece of Emotional Intelligence is self-regulation, which is the ability of an individual to control his emotions, curb his negative impulsive responses, and to think before expressing his emotions.

A person should thus learn to suspend judgment in any particular situation and think carefully before acting. For example, when an individual gets depressed because of the words uttered by someone else, the person should first be conscious that he is experiencing depression. He should then question the reason why he is in such a damaging emotional state. The next step would be to analyze his impulses and reflect upon whether his emotional reactions will be constructive or destructive. Despair is a very harmful emotion. The person needs to learn to detach himself from situations that harm his emotional state and then develop his logical thinking skills. The individual who involves himself emotionally in all situations will tend to have extreme emotional responses. Therefore, a human being should not let a situation or another person alter his emotional state and elicit negative reactions.

Moreover, a person should practice controlling his or her emotions. It will be a challenge for somebody accustomed to resorting to destructive emotional states and behaviors to change their thought processes and foster positive thoughts and emotions. For example, if individuals experience negative feelings, like guilt or anxiety, they should think rationally and view the situation objectively. Only after carefully examining the circumstances can they then give their judgment and decision.

Furthermore, empathy is another component of emotional Intelligence. A person needs to understand different people's emotional setup and treat those people according to their emotional reactions. In doing so, an individual can easily read another person's emotional state and avoid being emotionally engaged in the situation. Emotionally intelligent people have a better attitude and outlook on life.

Conquering Your Inner Critic

Everyone has an inner critic. The voice tells you that the job you did might not have been so great after all and that you don't look perfect or shouldn't feel good about yourself. Some let the voice get too strong, and this can quickly wreck your self-esteem.

It is normal to have some spells that are worse than others, but when your critic becomes the predominant voice in your head, it's time to learn how to conquer it.

The first step is realizing what your points of insecurity are. Journaling can help you pinpoint these aspects, as can gauging your mood at specific points during the day using useful scales such as the Rosenberg Self-Esteem Scale. Checking your self-esteem before a project and then again after can help you see if your work is bringing you down, or maybe your self-esteem grows after completing a household chore. Recognizing these patterns is an essential first step to owning and controlling your inner critic.

The next step is learning how to accept your flaws and let go of your failures. It sounds easy in theory, but in practice, it is actually challenging. You may find it helpful to interrupt your thoughts midstream before they become persistent. Have a list of things you are proud of, especially things about the situation, which can help you when the doubts start creeping in. If you feel as though you're about to start criticizing yourself, think of the items on your list that make you proud and focus on them until the doubts begin to subside.

A final step to conquer your inner critic happens when the first two steps are performed consistently and become habits. It is more of a change in your way of thinking. After applying the first two steps, the final step is somewhat self-fulfilling because you will naturally start to find the positive in what you've accomplished and minimized what you formerly saw as flaws. You'll find that the more you consciously review and assess your feelings, the more control you'll have over them. Knowing what makes you react negatively to a situation helps you realize what you need to do to avoid or fix the feelings quickly rather than dwelling on them, which is so common.

Overall, your inner critic is a stubborn nemesis that can be overcome with repetitive training to learn how to calm and quiet the nagging that many of us are so used to. Exercises can help silence the critic as well as increase your self- understanding. The exercises can help you become a better- rounded person and help in your everyday battle with your critic.

Practice, Practice, Practice

When looking to change your life and become the person you want to be, there is nothing like practice. Many people associate the practice with just sports or education, but practice applies to every aspect of life and can be invaluable in becoming who you want to be. Nobody can change overnight, and practice can be applied to every aspect of life to help you become the best version of yourself.

Practice doesn't have to be a person just repeating the same action over and over again; it can happen on paper or while playing out scenarios in your head. Lists and realizing what path one needs to follow are good ways to induce practice in your head and think ahead to what you'll do when confronted with a particular situation. Living through situations before they happen can be great social practice and help you think on your feet to don't freeze in critical life situations.

Preparedness can be seen as a helpful form of practice. Writing out what you want and figuring out the best way to accomplish your goals is also a perfect way to practice since you can't physically practice the steps day after day. The writing and planning will make it seem like you have practiced in person, though, as you will be prepared for many scenarios because you thought them through ahead of time. Dry runs can happen with drills if the provisions are available, or even something as simple as holding a conversation with yourself in the mirror can help prepare and practice for many different situations.

When you practice it every day, you'll be surprised at how it can infiltrate and help other aspects of your life. Knowing that quickly going over something in your head and playing out different outcomes can help prepare you for many different social interactions. Then people will notice that you are more comfortable and confident.

Of course, sometimes, practice is physical rather than mental. If you want to be a knitter, you'll knit until it becomes second nature, and that's the entire purpose of practicing both mentally and physically--to turn specific actions into muscle memory. The more you perform a task, the more naturally it comes afterward, and therefore, the more of an expert you become.

Practice really does make perfect. Making sure you know what you want and then dedicating time to practice. The practice is an essential step in becoming an expert in whatever you'd like to be an expert in.

HOW TO BUILD SELF-DISCIPLINE

Building self-discipline is not as hard as your mind might have been conditioned to believe, though it will not come without some efforts and commitment. Here are some tested and trusted techniques you can adopt to help you build and maintain self-discipline.

Hold Yourself Accountable Today

Individuals who lack self-discipline often don't retain accountability. To hold yourself accountable gives you conviction and warrants you to take responsibility for outcomes that occur. Avoid playing the blame game, as that is merely giving yourself excuses. Pointing the finger at someone else does nothing to empower you. Even if you feel that someone else has affected your performance, take responsibility, and make beneficial changes so that the person cannot affect your future feelings and performance.

You must learn to take chief responsibility for what you do and don't accomplish in life to claim your power. People who have a strong sense of willpower know that it will likely not get done if they do not accomplish something themselves. You must cast aside the defeatist attitude and the need to blame others for your shortcomings. Even though we cannot control everything that happens to us as human beings, we can control our reactions. Once you claim your power, you can take charge and move ahead.

Understand Where You Draw Inspiration and What Puts Your Light Off.

You have things that trigger your weaknesses and things that feed your significant strengths. Discovering things that bring out the best in you and bringing your weakest points to the fore will go a long way to building your self-discipline, a very simple and easy one. It means you must commit some time to learn more about yourself. Building self-discipline boils down to overcoming your strongest negative urges, cravings, and desires.

So, knowing what lowers your ability to resist your desire for the things you are trying to eliminate from your life and avoiding them will go a long way to help you achieve your self-discipline goal. If you have a problem keeping your hands-off junk foods, fries, sugary foods, and all other foods you have been advised to stay away from, make sure you avoid situations that could make you unable to resist them. We all have our time of weakness. Regardless how disciplined you are, there are times when you will find yourself unable to resist things you would usually resist without much effort on a typical day. If very disciplined people can be vulnerable to such occasional weaknesses, so can you. As you grow in maturity, your ability to inspire yourself to action grows.

For example, say that one of your goals is to lose weight and eat healthier. The best way to avoid taking foods that will make your entire weight loss diet plan a waste is to make sure such foods are not found anywhere near your kitchen or anywhere in your home. The moment you make the mistake of allowing such food items into your home, a day will come when you will be unable to resist the craving for them. It also applies to situations where you are trying to quit your addiction to alcohol or drugs. The only way you can escape the periods of intense cravings is by getting rid of all drinks or drugs from your home, office, or wherever you spend most of your time.

Your environment and the people play significant roles when fighting to get rid of certain habits and build self-discipline. You must make sure you are not surrounded by people who will try to talk you out of your self-discipline building project. Instead, surround yourself with motivators such as positive quotes, stories about the benefits of becoming self-discipline, stories of men and women who ended up achieving some great feats in life because they were self-disciplined, etc. One quick tip to help you on this journey is to know your weakest points and avoid them. One way to learn your weakest points is to pay attention to details that point out your greatest demoralizers. Think about the things you do and lose interest in pursuing your goals.

Think about what makes you feel like quitting and what makes you feel like giving it your all until your goal has been achieved. Think about the places, people, and scenarios that kill your passion for firing on. The moment you can pinpoint your significant detractors, you will be able to avoid them and become more self-disciplined.

Set A Goal

Every outstanding achievement in life begins with setting a feasible goal. You have to get in the habit of setting goals is that you become more self-disciplined. You can train yourself to act by forming an attainable goal. In setting a goal to become more self-disciplined, you must consider several factors, such as your most dominant traits, habits, significant strengths, and weaknesses. Things you have become addicted to, and things you would want to change in your life, etc. Your goal should have a date for beginning your efforts to increase your self-discipline level and a date by which you must have improved your level of self-discipline drastically.

We can give you a piece of straightforward advice to take this part as the theory of self-discipline. However, if you want to build your self-discipline, to put this theory into practice is mandatory. Remember, practice makes the Master. It will be necessary that you, after reading this book, stand up and start working on your goals. I guess that while you were reading this book, several goals and dreams unfulfilled crossed your mind, followed by the question: "why did I not do that?" Well, let us tell you, you still have time to reach some of your goals. The first thing you have to do is remember all the dreams you had and have in mind to make come true. The process of setting a goal includes the factor of putting feet on the ground. Please select only those goals that are feasible that you can accomplish in a short time. You can choose more complicated goals; nonetheless, you must be convinced that you must work on it. Once you go to bed, think about the goals you wanted to accomplish, for example, studying a career, constructing a wooden table, get a job, start your own business, anything. The idea is to put into practice the habit of self-discipline. We recommend you to select first a short-term goal to start.

Define A Set Personal and Career Goals for Your Life

Once you can set a single goal for yourself and follow- through, you should start developing a set of goals for your life. Self-disciplined people often have a bunch of goals that motivate and guide them in the path to progress. If you lack a clear set of goals for your life, it will be much more frustrating to maintain a self-disciplined attitude. Your goals give you a mission for each day that you live. The idea of reaching the goal destination can set your heart aflame and full of passion for living.

Break Your Goals Down

One of the best tactics that you can use to reach success is to break your goals into small objectives that you can work towards. Sometimes, a particular goal may seem daunting when it is looked at as a whole and a single destination. Still, if you break it down into small objectives, you may be quite surprised to see that you can advance towards them a little each day and that the goal is more attainable than you thought. By breaking your goals down to daily or weekly tasks, you can be satisfied knowing that you are diligently working towards your goals and dreams when you engage in every task.

Start with Baby Steps

When it comes to building self-discipline, you must begin with simple baby steps; you can easily learn to practice and move on to more complicated steps as you record improvements. Building your self-discipline, like every other necessary lifestyle change in life, will not happen overnight.

Building your self-discipline could be likened to building your muscles-both requires time, effort, patience, and perseverance. Things are not going to change because you have made some little efforts to affect some character changes the same way your muscles will not bulge out after a few workouts or muscle building exercises.

The more you spend time learning the techniques you could adopt to become a more disciplined you and putting what you learn into practice, the more you become self-disciplined. Just like you stand the risk of experiencing setbacks and possible injuries by attempting multiple muscle-building stunts. At the early stage of your practices, you will undoubtedly be shooting yourself in the leg when you try to become self- disciplined all at once.

The best way to start building your self-discipline is to make up your mind to do whatever you have to do to become a more disciplined you. Taking baby steps in this context implies attempting the little task first, achieving them convincingly before attempting the bigger ones. It will amount to the same indiscipline you are trying to do away with if you try to take on the harder tasks before the easier ones.

If you are trying to go to the gym to bulge out or try to lose weight, you must workout with simple routines if you're starting. Those baby steps are the little activities you have to regularly do day after day to improve significantly once time goes by.

Consider Counseling and Professional Help

In some cases, your self-discipline may not seem strong enough to help you overcome the issues you have in life. If you are experiencing with a very serious or life-threatening bad habit, you will probably need to acquire a trained professional's services to help you through it. Do not be afraid to talk to someone and to reach out. If you don't, the bad habits or addictions can make you lose control or even your life.

Suppose you can get help from a private or public counselor, a medical professional, or even an organization that offers aid. If you belong to a church, you can speak to a ministry member, a church leader, or your pastor to help encourage you. The point is not to take in the battle alone when there are people around you who can help you out.

Even in situations where you can get professional help, they will empower you to make better choices if you find it difficult to empower yourself. If you gain professional help from authorities, you can gain what is necessary to overcome addictions of any kind that can destroy the level of self- discipline you have and make you feel like a failure when you are not. Do not allow bad habits or addictions to rob you of your destiny. You worth it to be in control of your life and have the best that life has to offer you.

THE CONCEPT OF NOT KNOWING

"I don't let go of my thoughts. I meet them with understanding. Then they let go of me." -BYRON KATIE.

As you walk on the path of self-acceptance, you will often notice that thoughts, beliefs, concepts, and every form of information can never feel enough. As you obtain more ideas, some ideas seem left out. You have to differentiate between the information you need and the material you need to let go of. Our minds are complex. They can be either distorted or refined with information. Our job is to stay conscious and courageous – to be courageous enough to shun poisonous notions and silence destructive echoes from our thoughts. Information can do two things; it can make or mar you. Sensitivity is paramount in every stage of life. Sensitive in the sense that you can never really know all, so take comfort in knowing that you only need to access a few thoughts, meanings, concepts, and ideas at most stages of your life. You are not obligated to lend your ear to every detail; you only have to welcome healthy details. It is okay to allow specific thoughts to fly past simply. Allow them to take flight far away from your heart. Because we are sometimes sabotaged by our thoughts and the things we hear from our inner voices.

We Are All Plagued by Our Ill-Thoughts

As we listen to words that buzz around our minds and the gossip of other people, we become fragile, defensive, and vulnerable. Be courageous enough to let such things go!

Before you begin the self-acceptance journey, it is worth realizing that people in your circle may claim to be oblivious of your transformation and are likely to preserve memories of your old flawed nature. Maybe they don't want you to change. Or, perhaps, they don't understand. So, don't be disturbed if they keep expecting the old you, but ignore the details of their words.

Generally, information as a whole is critical, a man can get into trouble for what he knows, and the same man can be celebrated for what he knows. You have to be intelligent enough to draw the line between what you should accept into your heart and what you should discard.

Our views, beliefs, and perception tend to remain fixed most of the time. They are very rigid. Their rigidity effectively shuts our minds from considering other possibilities, including considering views that don't resonate with us.

When you open your heart to unnecessary details, you will realize that you are standing in your way to freedom and success in time.

Take Courage

Do not bow to every myth. Question them often, see if they are acceptable, disposable, or destructive. Question the thought that appears to be true - thoughts that may even feel like a part of your identity. It is possible for thoughts you don't act on to exist in your mind without harming you; it all depends on how you position them. The actuality that they exist does not make them valid. What validates those thoughts is your ability to consistently "think on them" and act on them.

To maintain stillness and not allow our thoughts to control our actions is admirable. When we find the courage to be still and go within, we can meet the freedom that lives on the other side. It is not your place to know everything: it is not your place to gather every detail. You don't have to try and become an omnipresent god. We only see a small glimpse of reality, but that fraction is enough to bring us the positive results we need. The chances are, you'll never get the full picture of life, no matter how much you try. So stop stretching to amass all the details, instead search and grab what is significant.

Free Yourself from Self-Orientation

Rhonda Byrne once said, "Our body is an infinite field of unfolding possibilities, a creative force." There is no dividing line to what we can achieve if we acquire strength, power, knowledge, or skills. It isn't that the doors of opportunity have closed, but that we have shut ourselves out.

The reason you wake up feeling curious is that the universe is trying to open up its wonders and possibilities to you. It is saying, "There is so much knowledge you have not accessed yet."

This thought can be fascinating, making you feel curious and desperate for knowledge. But to grasp, one must be humble enough to admit ignorance. It's the order of things. A student must feel void, needy, and curious to study widely, research, and go the extra mile to acquire knowledge. So we need to get into the core dynamics of our mind. That's how to relinquish your pseudo-self. Your pseudo-self is the personality inside you that makes you feel like you already have enough and that you do not need any new concept or philosophy.

Reinforce What Works for You

Not all information is healthy for you, and not all philosophy is meant for your consumption. However, although your life will be better off when it excludes some details, the information that can improve you is the information you need. So, do not let ego or insensitivity cripple the appetite for learning. Liberate yourself from the oppression of pride; know that you don't know all and that you need refueling.

The secret to growth is humility. Humility is a sense of emptiness. The feeling that there is more for you out there that you haven't yet discovered. When people make five-to-ten- year plans, they don't just see the pride of being a successful person; they imagine the number of things they need to accomplish to reach their goal.

Decide where you want to be in the upcoming five or ten years. Ask yourself, "What can I do to be this person? What attitude can I exhibit to take the shape of my future self?" You have to carry out a self-surgery, take out those elements that drag you down, and cultivate habits that enable you to rise above your current self.

Master Your Internal World

Deep inside us, we know that there is something to take hold of, something grand. No matter the magnitude of goals we set, we still get to that level where we are unsatisfied with our current situation, and so, we are inspired to invest more strength or energy into trying to attain or grasp that which isn't yet ours. We often find ourselves in that position of "needing a little more," but we sometimes forget that our internal world has a role to play in our effort to attain or achieve. Your internal world encompasses all the things that go on in your mind, beliefs, concepts, and prospects.

Examine your internal faculty - the thoughts and beliefs you have about yourself and others. What beliefs do you have with yourself and the people around you? The Universe answers to you based on the thoughts you are holding in your mind. As your mind opens itself to knowing, your body will readjust and conform to that change. There is a connection between what goes on in our minds and what manifests in our bodies. Your mind, in a way, functions as your spiritual dimension.

The best way to want more is to believe you do not know. Knowledge is naturally restricted when there is a stoppage in the journey of learning. We need some daily or short supply of intellects, skills, and knowledge to stay mentally rich and able to live the life we desire.

Admission of Ignorance Opens the Doorway For "Knowing"

We want the right relationship, we want the right jobs, we want the best of material possessions, but we are often afraid to admit that we do not know how to get those things. We are usually in a loop, a shallow, confused state, where we are oblivious of the big picture or how what we have imagined and dreamed will manifest.

We are in this state because we are shying away from acknowledging that we are void, void of knowledge, void of direction, void of perception. What you do not know is always looking for a way to locate you, but, sometimes, we are clouded by fear or ego, so much that we do not open our hearts to admit that we honestly do not know.

When you open your soul to the versatile nature of the universe, life becomes limitless. You will see the depth of possibilities that you should take part in, and the more you relish in this consciousness, "knowing more" becomes effortless.

Model your life to be impacted, and do not let expectations deprive you of life's joy. So, expect disappointments, expect failure and expect to be denied. When these things happen, don't feel demoralized; feel energized to push further. Similarly, do not expect your mentors to teach you; teach yourself. Do not let your friends guide you; guide yourself. Do not expect people to do favors for you. YOU ARE THE TRUE MASTER of yourself, and expectations can limit you.

There are no particular way things should be done, so do not also expect scenarios to always play out in your favor. Open your heart to the odd and fair side of reality.

So, note that there is no one-way pattern; there are several-way patterns. Everything is not as it seems. There is a second picture of every reality you see; it is called the "unforeseen reality." So before settling for thought, check the validity of it.

What you think about the world inside your head may not be an accurate representation of the real world.

"Not-knowing" is not an excuse for passivity. It merely means you're opening up to other things, things that exist but are unrevealing. There are "the other side possibilities." Like thinking about the possibility of not reaching that goal or the potential of reaching the goal. There may be a backlash, true. But there is also the chance of winning. If you think in this direction, you will open your consciousness to new things, and by so doing, you activate the consciousness into acquiring useful knowledge.

For you not to get this concept twisted, the "Not-knowing" should make you an optimist and not a pessimist. It doesn't mean you should have a myopic view of yourself and others. It helps you let go of the ideas about what makes you perfect while still retaining your confidence and self-esteem.

It makes you live without other people's validations or vague perceptions of you. It makes you feel positive about the personal beliefs you've built for yourself. As you do things, you will discover new strengths, new powers, and new revelations about your abilities. It means that the concept of "not-knowing" abruptly leads to personal development.

THE TRUTH WILL SET YOU FREE

This guide's entire focus is about helping you understand who you are to be better at being yourself. Defining who you are. Understanding, valuing, and honoring who you are and doing all the work required to make you better at just being yourself. No matter what mask or what persona you try to hide behind, your real self knows the inner truth. For your inner truth to shine through, you need to value yourself and see what you are worth. Otherwise, you'll never indeed be happy because you're trying to live a life that is not true to who you are.

As the name would imply, the inner truth is something that comes from within you. It is a truth that resonates with you more than anything else. When you are living by your inner truth, you feel compelled to act. Life has a purpose, and you're filled with passion. You're ignited with positive feelings and aspirations. Inner truth is not something you build over time. It is something that happens when you start to embrace yourself and be comfortable in your own skin.

Steps to Step into Your Truth

One of the reasons your inner truth is probably suppressed right now is doubt. Your attitude is the environment just you build for yourself. It can be any state you want it to be. If you create an environment for yourself that is positive, then your attitude and outlook will mirror that. If you build a negative environment, your attitude and perspective are going to mirror that too. The question you need to ask yourself is, what kind of environment do I want for myself so my inner truth shines through? You need to develop an attitude that stays true to who you are and not tries to be something you are not. You may have role models and other personalities whose success you aspire to emulate, but you are still your own person. Use that success as a model for improving yourself, but avoid setting unrealistic expectations in trying to be something that you are not. Set expectations based on your capabilities, situation, and what options are available to you because that is what you've got to work with because that's the first step towards working on your inner truth.

We find it so hard to release our inner truth because we're too judgmental. We're too hard on ourselves. We color our reality unnecessarily with ideas and thought patterns of how we "think" things should be. When you're not living following your inner truth, it's impossible to live your best life. We place too much stress on external validation. We crave for possession of the wrong things, like pleasing others or materialism. We're far too distracted by what's happening externally that we forget to focus on what's going on internally. Most people have a hard time focusing on their inner truth because they're too distracted and too busy pursuing the wrong ideals. If you asked them, they don't know who they are without the fancy house, the flashy cars, the fine clothes or expensive watches. That's because they're not tuned in to their inner truths.

Try this exercise. Ask yourself, "Who am I?". How would you describe yourself? Ask the same question to anyone else. "Who are you?" How would they describe themselves? I'm the boss. I'm a wife. I'm a mother. I'm a father. I'm a husband. I'm a brother or sister. I'm a lawyer. I'm a doctor. Those titles are not answering the question, though. Those titles are merely describing the role you play, not who you are on the inside. To start discovering your inner truth, you need to strip yourself of these titles and these ideals. There is nothing more important in life than to be authentic, genuine, and real. To stay true to yourself instead of pandering to other people or pretending to be someone we are not. Being true to ourselves doesn't mean we must be defensive. It does not mean we need to be resistant to change. It is entirely possible to be your authentic self yet make the necessary adjustments to have better relationships with the people around us.

Only when you stop defending yourself against the world and not resisting change will your authentic self and inner truth emerge. You will only fully embrace your inner truth when there is no longer any fear of losing your identity. You must be willing to embrace change, be open to it because part of stepping into your inner truth is welcoming the willingness to grow and change.

It is how you need to begin stepping into your inner truth:

Ask Yourself, "Is This Really Me?" - Observe how you behave in certain situations. Look at the things you do and the things you think you should do. In everything you do, ask yourself, "Is this really me? How do I feel about that? What's my intuition telling me?". To live according to your inner truth, your actions should match your morals, values, and beliefs. Many people go through life swept up in different versions of themselves that they have forgotten all about their inner truths along the way. They don't consciously pay attention to what they are doing, so it's time to practice mindfulness and start paying more attention to what you do.

Care Less About What Others Think - When you start to care a little less about what others think and prioritize the way you think and feel, that's the moment you're going to be free. At the core, so many of us rely on external validation by others because we believe what they offer us can have true, lasting value. Whether you realize it or not, somewhere deep down inside, you believe that this person you're interacting with can give you something and that "something" is so meaningful and valuable that you need it. It is also why we become people pleasers. You want approval and for your self-image to be validated by others.

Releasing Resistance - Don't let fear be the reason you resist accepting and embracing yourself. When you originate from a place of acceptance, you're better able to say, "Yes, I accept this is who I am" and "Yes, I accept this is happening right now." Step into your inner truth by releasing resistance to change. Embrace what is going on around you and within you. Accept rather than resist, and your emotions will eventually settle down without excessive negativity.

Listening to Your Emotions - This one is essential. Emotions are not the enemy. Emotions are signposts and messages from yourself. These emotions come from the subconscious that tells you when something is not right if what you're feeling is negative. Instead of rejecting your emotions, you need to listen to them. Ask them what's the matter. Ask why you feel the way that you do. Could it have anything to do with the fact that you're not living by your inner truth? You see, the inner truth within us wants to come out. It is screaming to be let out, and if we stop long enough to listen, that's when we start to see the signs we might have overlooked before. If you're experiencing many negative emotions, you need to ask yourself why they are there and trace it back to their source. Your emotions are there for a reason. Listen to them, and they will point out which parts of yourself need healing the most so you can live according to your inner truth.

Trust in Your Opinions - It's another way of saying believe in yourself. When you've made a conscious decision about something, trust that you've made the best decision possible for yourself. Trust that you believe this is the best course of action with the information you have to work with and stand by those opinions. If you don't stand firm and set boundaries, other people will come in and push their opinions on you, squashing down your inner truth. If you let them, they'll trample all over you and drain you of everything you have. Without proper boundaries, there's no stopping them from taking advantage of you every step of the way. Borders matter in any interpersonal relationship; you have to maintain a healthy dynamic between you and the other person. If you don't want your inner truth to be drowned out, then you need these boundaries in your life.

Don't Filter Your Personality - There's only so much filtering of your personality that you can do before it eventually takes its toll on you. When you present a filtered version of yourself, you're never going to be happy. You're always going to live in fear that people are not going to like you or accept you for who you are. Presenting this filtered version of yourself can quickly become hard work and exhausting. It's impossible to please everyone, and the sooner you accept this reality, the easier it will be to start making decisions based on what you think will be best for you and your inner truth. If you are basing your choices on the information you have and what you're going to be most comfortable with, that's all you can do.

Don't Feel Pressured - Don't let anyone make you feel pressured into rushing being someone you're not. Don't let anyone stress you into making decisions that your inner truth is not comfortable with. Some decisions, especially the big ones, take time to process and work through, and you have the right to take as much time as you need to come to what you believe will be the best decisions. You don't want people in your life who are not going to accept you for who you are and respect the decisions you have made, so if you lose a couple of people along the way because of this, they might not be the right people for you to begin with.

HEALING AND SELF-ACCEPTANCE WITH EMOTIONAL HONESTY

Emotional honesty is our way of healing ourselves when we are emotionally wounded. Emotional wounds, unlike wounds to our body, are mainly invisible. They are easy to ignore, deny, and overlook. Unattended emotional wounds are dangerous to us because they weaken our sense of self- acceptance. The pain from our unhealed, unattended wounds remains with us even when we fool ourselves that it doesn't hurt. We have a critical choice in life: To either suffer emotional distress by pretending we aren't hurt or try to recover from our wounding experiences by accepting each injury and the true pain that accompanies it. Acceptance of our painful feelings leads to genuine self-acceptance. Our self-acceptance then strengthens our ability to recover from, not fear, future emotional injuries. Having hurt feelings is inevitable: recovering from them is not. The difference is emotional honesty.

While none of us is emotionally honest all the time, each of us can learn to recognize when we are being self-deceptive about recognizing when our feelings are painful and distressing to us. There is no simple shortcut for achieving self-acceptance. It comes from honoring our feelings even when they are threatening and upsetting. In the process of emotional honesty, we are always seeking the real meaning of our emotional distress when we are wounded. We are continually learning about our self-deception, our fears, and our vulnerability. We are not given self-acceptance by our parents, mates, or others: we must work at it. We must take responsibility for healing ourselves by honoring our hurt. How we react to painful experiences, to a large extent, determines how self-accepting we can be.

Many of us seek help from therapists to guide us on this journey for self-acceptance. David Viscott, the author of The Making of a Psychiatrist (1972) and several of the recommended books listed in Appendix IV, states that "the principal directive of psychotherapy is to help the patient become more truthful about his feelings." From practicing psychiatry for over 30 years, he concludes, "In nearly all the therapeutic breakthroughs I have seen, it was the acceptance of some past concealed truth (about feelings) that allowed healing to begin." He emphasizes that emotional honesty comes from recognizing and lowering defenses, not from eliminating them. Being aware of defenses and pretenses that mask vulnerability allows us to accept being wounded without being damaged or feeling devastated. Resilient persons recover from their wounds and emotional distress more readily.

They have learned that, in the long run, emotional honesty is the best policy for having healthy, accepting relationships with themselves and others. Emotional honesty is difficult to practice, for it requires both the undoing of self-deception and the development of our ability to accurately sense, identify, and claim our real feelings—from pain to joy. Knowing what we feel requires naming what we feel when we feel it. It is difficult and takes courage to carefully listen to our pain to name it and honor it, but this process improves with practice. In his 1996 book, The Art of Forgiving, Lewis Smedes emphasizes that this is a learned rather than a natural process:

Philosophers have said that all education aims to learn how to give things their right names.

By learning to name our pain, we limit its potentially destructive influence on our self-acceptance and others' acceptance. Naming feelings that otherwise remain vague and threatening gives us the power to claim them. By listening to and respecting their message, we can see why emotional injuries trigger a fear of being unlovable or unacceptable. Embracing painful feelings with respect enables us to honor and accept them as part of us. By owning feelings, we more completely accept ourselves, including our vulnerability and our human capability to feel hurt.

Rabbi Harold Kushner, in his 1997 book, How Good Do We Have to Be? (Appendix IV), notes that "Only when we know that we are acceptable and lovable will we be able to change the things we don't like about ourselves." Treating pain as an indictment of our character leads to spending a lifetime looking for acceptance from others to make up for our perceived unworthiness's corrosive fear and shame.

Self-acceptance is more than having high self-esteem, self-confidence, or receiving "approval" from others. As Michael Nichols says in No Place to Hide (Appendix IV), "Self- confidence is particular to a situation; self-acceptance is who we are no matter what the situation. How we feel about ourselves affects what we feel free to do—and our tolerance for making mistakes and enduring failure."

Self-acceptance involves knowing and trusting that we can recover by being with our pain until it is defined when we are injured. Restricting our pain limits it to the specific wound, rather than allowing it to threaten our very being. We need not carry lifelong grudges for past assaults, for we were only wounded, not permanently damaged. If we can name and tame the fear and shame of being hurt, we can recover and move on. David Viscott, whose insights have been an inspiration for this book, says that emotional honesty "allows you to believe in yourself, accept criticism without blaming others, and take failure without being crushed" (Appendix IV, 1996). Michael Nichols points out that we need to recognize that for healing to take place: "We are vulnerable. Simply dropping defenses exposes us once again to the pain that was the reason for erecting the defenses in the first place. We can begin to relax the grip of shame by reaching out . . .taking risks, opening ourselves up to other people—but it's important to realize that we will get hurt along the way."

Paying attention to one's pain isn't wallowing in self-pity or overemphasizing it to get attention. Respectfully attending to our hurt allows us to more precisely define and limit the emotional wound as an experience, not an indictment of our character. Respecting, rather than ignoring, emotional wounds keep us from putting up a stoic front and saying to ourselves, "If I don't pay any attention to it, maybe the pain will go away." The more we respect our hurt, the more we respect ourselves. We can then treat our injury with respect and self- compassion to recover from its painful effects.

The four core wounding experiences—loss, rejection, betrayal, and humiliation—tell us what is important to us, what we have lost, and how much we need others. It is essential to have trusting relationships, and how fearful we are of losing our humanity by being humiliated.

The OATH of Emotional Honesty

Despite growing up in a family where emotional dishonesty was the rule, you can set new rules for yourself, your own family, and future generations. These new rules can become a new family tradition. These four simple rules, which summarize main points from this book, may be used as an OATH to commit yourself to deal honestly and non- judgmentally with feelings—yours and others. It involves recognizing the often-imperceptible danger signals of feeling unlovable and unacceptable whenever you suffer emotional wounds. Upholding the OATH means striving to be more emotionally aware and honest, even if you cannot always achieve these goals. It takes a commitment to yourself to accept your feelings as an essential part of yourself. The OATH is easy to learn since the first letters of each element spell the word OATH:

- Owning feelings
- Acknowledging feelings

- Trusting feelings

- Honoring feelings

Owning Feelings

When we own our feelings, significantly hurt feelings arising from wounding experiences, we respect and take responsibility for them, for they tell us who we are. By taking responsibility for what we feel, we don't need to blame others for our emotional pain. By owning our feelings, we refuse to distance ourselves from them. We will not turn away from painful feelings by treating them as orphans, nor hide our hurt as a shameful sign of weakness. By owning feelings, we affirm that we can experience pain and joyful responses to life's experiences.

Acknowledging Feelings

When we can name our feelings, we acknowledge them and give them reality and importance in our life. We recognize what we feel when we feel it and become more emotionally present. By refusing to judge painful feelings as "bad," we acknowledge that to be vulnerable and hurt is part of being human. This acknowledgment also distinguishes between what we feel and what we think, believe, do, or value. Feelings are real and exist incontrovertibly as part of us, even if we sometimes choose to ignore or discount them. David Viscott (in his 1992 book, Emotionally Free) says, "Healing begins when you tell the truth about your hurt." He says it is not our anger over the hurt we need to get in touch with and express; it is the meaning of the hurt itself.

Trusting Feelings

Knowing our emotional truth enables us to trust ourselves. Feelings are emotional responses we have to live. They are important messages we need to trust, for they tell us what we care about. While we may not always select to act upon our emotional truth, we won't summarily deny it, either. We may not always have the courage to risk being honest about what we feel, but we will not degrade the significance of these vital inner experiences as if they are not an essential part of us.

Honoring Feelings

We honor feelings by allowing them to stay with us long enough to know their meaning and significance. We neither need to be ashamed of them nor apologize for what we feel, for this is our reality. Honoring the pain from losses and other troubling experiences enables us to keep feelings that tell us how much we love, care about, and have compassion for ourselves and others. By honoring feelings, we are neither too fearful of grieving and healing our pain nor too wary of celebrating and honoring our joy freely.

WHAT IS EFFECTIVE GOAL-SETTING?

Giving yourself goals to reach in your life can allow you to feel that you have a purpose. When you create realistic and beneficial goals, you will always have something to look forward to. With each goal set, remember that there will be a beginning, middle, and end — it takes commitment and hard work on your end.

Every successful person you meet is likely to have a list of goals they are currently working toward. If you have goals that you have been trying to reach or have yet to make any for yourself, now is the time to accomplish them. When you can check items off your to-do list, this allows you to have a huge boost in confidence. You will feel great about yourself when you see what you are truly capable of.

What most people forget about goal-setting is that the goals need to be realistic. It is a nice goal to want to become a millionaire, but you will only be setting yourself up for failure if this is the only goal you create. Don't refrain from having these big goals, but understand it will take smaller steps to get there. Some examples of effective goal-setting in this situation might be starting a savings account, getting a side job, and working on cutting down your expenses. No matter what goals you have, even the biggest ones, try to break down the steps into direct and straightforward tasks.

Think about where you are in your life right now. Consider if you are in a career that suits you best. Would you change jobs if you could? Your personal life should be considered, too. Do you plan on growing your family? Don't forget about your own personal happiness. Is there anything that you would like to have more of in your life to maintain your best lifestyle possible? When you take a realistic look at the things you already have and what you want to have, this will give you some framework for creating a brand-new list of goals to reach. Remember that realistic means what you can actually see yourself accomplishing with the means that you currently have. While this can change in the future, you need to work with the resources you have right now.

Separate your goals by short-term and long-term. Your short-term goals should be the ones that you can see yourself accomplishing within the year. These goals are likely going to be simple, smaller things, but that is okay. Any accomplishment is one that is worth being proud of yourself for. Your long-term goals can consist of things you want for your immediate future; think within the upcoming five years. When you can separate your goals in this way, this will keep you on top of the things that you should be prioritizing. If you do not differentiate between them, you might find yourself feeling overwhelmed at where to start.

Each action that you take toward completing a goal should have a clear beginning and end. It will prevent you from doing too many things at once. When you leave open-ended steps for yourself, this is going to lead you to distractions. Have a transparent idea of the process that you are going to take toward accomplishing your goals. Break each one down into exact steps, remembering that you cannot get from point

A to point B without working on the things in between. Even if you have to do something different every day, know that this effort will be worth it in the long run.

Reaching Goals

As you go forth in accomplishing your goals, remember to create a method that works for you. While there are countless tips and strategies that you can try, all of them are not going to work for you. It will be a period of self-discovery as you experiment with these tips until you find the ones that serve you. This process is great, and it will allow you to learn a lot about yourself and your lifestyle. Many people do not realize that success begins with a fair amount of trial and error; no one has it figured out from the beginning.

Accountability does not have to be seen in a negative context. You might know with the term from instances where you have made a mistake. While it is important to take accountability for your actions during these times, you need to recognize that you are accountable during other times. Recognize that accountability during a time when you are aiming for goals will keep you true to yourself. It is a way for you to recognize that you are still doing your best and doing everything you can for yourself. Redefine the term and try to use it in an inspiring way.

Think about extremes. While your goals are likely not to put your life on the line, imagine if they did. Acknowledge what you would change if you had to reach these goals as if your life depended on it. While this can be an intense way to view your goals, sometimes, this is what it takes to jumpstart your motivation. Thinking this way gets you used to go through all of your options. People tend to give up if they are not presented with solutions that are convenient and easy. When you want to reach your goals, it isn't always going to be simple. You might have to take multiple steps to get there, but they will be worth it.

Balance the pros and cons. When you want to accomplish anything, you need to be driven to want it more than its challenges deter you. Everything worth fighting for will be challenging, but this doesn't mean you have to be in a negative mindset while you work on getting there. As you know, negativity is not good for your self-esteem. Try to keep your mindset as positive as possible, focusing on the results you wish to see.

Get feedback from someone you trust. While you might feel that you are doing everything you can to reach your goals, it helps to get an opinion from someone who cares about you. With their outside perspective, they might be able to shed some light on some things that you could be doing differently. If you want to be successful, being open to constructive criticism is a must. Know that it is not an attack on your abilities, but instead, a way for you to better yourself.

Know that your self-worth is not directly tied to your success. No matter how long it takes you to reach your goals or what you must do to get there, the process cannot make you a person who is deemed unworthy or not good enough. It is destined a journey, and it is going to involve many steps. You cannot expect to be handed all of the things you want most; that requires hard work and determination. Learn how to separate yourself from the things that you must do to reach your goals. Realize that you are still a valuable person, even if it takes you time to get there or if you have to try countless methods.

By learning how to separate yourself from these steps, you will rely on your confidence the entire time. It can be a foreign feeling to see yourself as an individual with great qualities rather than only a success or a failure. Think about how you would support someone you care about on their journey of reaching their goals. You would likely try to be as motivational as you can, encouraging them along the way. Know that you need to be this same person for yourself. Give yourself credit where credit is due. Celebrate your successes and keep yourself motivated to reach more goals. Don't take yourself too seriously, even when things won't seem to go your way. Many factors might be trying to bring you down, but you do not have to succumb to them.

BE THE REAL YOU AND STOP WORRYING ABOUT WHAT OTHER PEOPLE THINK

Life can be challenging. In a world with certain expectations of how you should look and how you should act, you feel like you are continually trying to fit in. You just want to be yourself, but how would the world see that? So, you try everything you can to fit into the world's standards, and you end up being something that you're not. Not only that, but you feel as though you could make a crucial mistake at any moment.

No Matter What, Be Yourself

If you're in a situation where you have no idea who you really are, now is the time to find out who that person deep down really is. When confronted with daily activities, don't put your censors on. Let what happens naturally happens. When you lower your guard and let yourself normally react to life, you will begin to see who the real you are. Let that person out. It is one of the first ways to become more confident in yourself!

Learn to Walk Away from Worldly Expectations and Set Your Own Pace

Sometimes it feels like everyone has a script that they need to follow to survive. If they don't follow it, something bad will happen. That's not true. Society tries to get us to act in specific ways. However, break free from those expectations. We're not saying go wild and do illegal things. Just don't conform to what society expects of you. You still have to follow the land rules and laws, but you don't have to be expected to fit into a societal mold that everyone else seems to come out of.

Surround Yourself with Those Who Value Who You are

Some people will like the person you really are on the inside. It's just a matter of letting that person show. Find those people who value you for who you are and make it a point to spend time with them. Breaking out of your shell can be difficult to do, but once people see the real you, they will value you for that.

Don't Take Criticism to Heart

Everyone will have an opinion of what you're doing and how you're acting. It's just the way it is. Sometimes that criticism is founded, but most times, it's a simple opinion that they want to express. Know when criticism is constructive and relevant. If you're sure that they are just trying to push their views upon you, then let that criticism go and continue to do what makes you who you are.

Realizing that you're beautiful is one of the first ways to be confident in who you are. We all have the habit of trying to fit into the world, making it impossible to be who we indeed are. How can we express confidence when we're hiding behind a mask? Let the real you out and learn to let people love you for who you are, not the way you want them to perceive you to be!

What Others Think is Irrelevant

Once you begin to show your confidence in who you are as a person, people will be eager to share their thoughts about that with you. Some are going to be encouraging, while others might be incredibly critical. Knowing what to take and what to leave behind can be difficult, especially if the opinions are from close to you.

Remove the Negative from Your Life

People and their criticisms can be incredibly negative. Since they have opinions, they will do whatever they can to make the world how they envision it. It might mean criticizing those who they feel are weaker than themselves and that they can force change in. Realize to identify these people in your life and let your confidence shine through when you're around them. If they see that they cannot push you around with their viewpoints, they will eventually stop trying. The key is to be confident that you're doing the right thing for you and not conforming to the negative people's expectations around you.

Know the Difference Between Constructive Criticism and Harmful Criticism

There is some criticism out there that is meant to be helpful. It might be challenging to figure out what that is at times because our first reaction to criticism is to feel hurt and defensive. However, you must learn to take a step back from your initial reaction and think about whether or not the criticism was meant to help you or hurt you. Confidence is a tool built with time, and if you let criticism tear you down, you won't see any progress in your life. Take what is constructive and leave all the other criticism behind you!

Not Letting Others' Comments Bother, You

Sometimes people can be unintentionally hurtful with their words. Even though they did not mean what came out of their mouths, it can still be a huge blow to your confidence. Learning to let the hurtful comments roll-off, you will bring you one step closer to feeling confident in yourself and what you're doing in life. Don't let other people dictate who you are because they have no filters on their mouths. Simply smile and continue on your way in the manner you know is right for you!

Being Confident in Yourself

If you learn to not listen to everything others have to say to you, you will find that you are more confident on your own. Being aware that people will try to mold you to their expectations and that you might not always have the same group of people in your life is just one step toward finding out who you are and being confident in that person. Remember, you are a strong, beautiful individual, and by finding your self-confidence, you can show the world much more than if you conform to society's standards!

You Can Do It and Believing You Can

Words have power. If you tell yourself that you can do it, you will begin to believe that you can do it. During the project, you might start to feel that it's impossible, but if you continue to tell yourself that you can do it, you can power through the task and finish it successfully. If you allow your thoughts to hinder your progress, you won't accomplish what you set out to do. No matter what happens, continue to tell yourself that you can do it!

Go into the Task with Full Energy and Knowing You Will Accomplish it

Going into a task full-force can help you to get through it more manageable. If you go into a project with a negative attitude, you will more than likely struggle through the task the entire time, and more than likely, you won't even finish what you started successfully. By focusing your energy, along with a positive mindset, upon the task before you, you can and will get what you set out to do done. Once you see that your positive mindset helps you achieve what you wish to accomplish, you will begin to find even more confidence in your abilities to do tasks correctly.

Don't Allow Negative Thoughts to Change Your Attitude

When someone struggles with self-esteem and lacks confidence, negative thoughts will often prevent a "can-do" attitude. However, you can take control of your thoughts and push the negativity away. By expressing positive insights amid the negative thoughts, you will find that positivity will reign. Let that be the driving force in your attitude, and don't allow negativity to change how you feel and what you wish to accomplish.

See it Through Until the End

Life has a way of giving obstacles in front of us. If we are already in a negative mindset, we will allow those obstacles to hinder our progress and leave the task unfinished. Even if you start to feel negative, push through until the task is complete. By seeing the finished product, you will begin to feel the confidence you lacked while facing the struggles. Knowing that you made it through a difficult time or task is a huge boost to help you feel more fulfilled and confident in yourself and your abilities!

Attitude is a driving force in whether or not we can accomplish things daily. By evaluating your attitude towards life and its tasks, you will get a better idea about what can be affecting your self-esteem and hindering your confidence. Nevertheless, if you go into each day with a "can-do" attitude, you will find that everything will become easier, and you will be able to accomplish what you put your mind to.

UNLOCK YOUR SUPERPOWERS

We all have inherent superpowers. We just need to identify these. You are also born with these superpowers. Maybe sometimes you used these powers, but you could not recognize it. If you observe, you'll find that when you need it, some of your special abilities automatically come into action.

Think about some everyday situations in life. If the exam is on the head, you read the whole year's syllabus in two days. If there is a catastrophe in the family, you spend two to three sleepless nights in the hospital. When there are any festivals and are excited about it, you show tremendous energy and work exceptionally. If you look towards your life, you will find many such examples to use your superpowers knowingly or unknowingly.

You have a powerful mind and a fantastic body. When the powers of these unite, you create wonders. We often talk about the powers, but have you realized the power of your body? Your body is also equipped with exclusive powers.

In this part, you'll know about the superpowers of your body and mind. Before speaking about the powers of the mind, we would like to tell you about your seven physical powers. If, for any reason, you think you are weak, know about these seven facts.

Seven Superpowers of The Body

Your bones are stronger than steel. By the age of 30, a human bone is stronger than most metals found in this world. A person can lift four times more weight than his weight. If the body is strengthened, then the bones can be up to five times stronger than the steel.

You can survive for two months without food. Experts believe that a person can survive without food for two months, which has been confirmed in the past. Many people lived easily for two months only by drinking water in abnormal conditions of life.

Our nose can recognize 50,000 different aromas and remember it; there is also a magical ability in the human nose. It can realize the 50,000 different smells and remember it. However, if there is no use, no one uses this ability.

There are 576-megapixel cameras in your eyes. Nowadays, smartphones come with high-tech cameras. Their capacity is in different megapixels ranging from 8 megapixels to 40-50 megapixels. Even a DSLR is up to 120 megapixels. In contrast, our eyes have a total of 576 megapixels camera. That's why we can see almost 10 million colors.

You can use the sound to 'see.' Bats are those animals who use the ears to see things. You also have such a capability. Many people who hit target blindly hear the voice and get an idea of the distance. If you train yourself for this, you can use this ability.

Your heart generates enough energy to drive a truck. Our heart produces so much energy in one day that a truck can be run up to 32 km. Believe it or not, this kind of exceptional energy flows in you.

You can use an 'adrenaline rush' to gain extraordinary power. You get an explosion of energy when you play an adventure game, such as bungee jumping, racing, or skydiving. This sudden flow of energy is known as an 'adrenaline rush.'

We can use this exceptional energy to achieve bigger things that we cannot achieve with the usual potential and strength. Every person has the skill to use his senses to the extended levels. Even if someone lacks any of his senses, he automatically finds other strong senses.

It's a law of nature. Therefore, even if you have any weaknesses in your body, there is no reason that you consider yourself weak. Check, you must have other surprisingly strong senses. Now we will tell you about the seven powers of mind that will not only awaken the powers of your mind but will also allow you to awaken your body's powers.

Seven exceptional powers of the mind:

Power of Attraction

You must have heard about the 'law of attraction.' It has become famous in the last few decades. However, it has always been one of the most significant powers of the human mind. Some people consider the law of attraction as a miracle; some people consider it a scientific process. You are free for your considerations, but the rule is very effective. Many successful people have witnessed this power in their lives. It is possible that you, too, have experienced it.

Our mind is like a powerful machine that works on special instructions. These instructions come through our internal thoughts. The speed of our mind is quick. We get 50 to 70 percent thoughts per day, which we do not think of being conscious. About 80 to 90 % of people with bad programming have more negative thoughts. Bringing positive thinking is the best way to use the law of attraction.

The rule of attraction states, 'In the universe, our mind acts like a magnet, and it attracts reality through the power of thoughts.' That's why your mindset has so much influence on your life. Your success-failure, happiness-grief, prosperity- impoverishment all depends on your thinking. That is why it is assumed that whatever your mind can conceive and believe, it can achieve. Your thinking is the biggest power. So, improve your mindset, have positive thoughts, and attract good things for yourself.

Power of Faith

Different people have different belief systems. They have faith in their gods, gurus, religion, or something else. Some people are spiritual, and some are atheists. However, you are free for your beliefs, but your external beliefs impact your inner personality. You are the most important person for yourself. So you have to believe in yourself. When you have an inner belief system, you can achieve everything.

After understanding the power of attraction, you know that your mind attracts things. You can attract whatever you want. So, believe that the greatest powers exist in you.

Have faith in your inner powers. If you believe in God, surrender yourself to his powers. He has given his powers inside you. You should use this. If you don't believe in God, have faith in yourself. Your inner powers, and you will get everything you want.

Faith has miraculous power. There are many examples in this world where people have achieved all because of their faith. Persistence is born with faith, and it always brings out the best from you.

Power of Correspondence

The power of correspondence directly connects your inner and outer world. According to this rule, your inner world will affect your outside world and, in the same way, your outer world affects your inner world. That is, if you are happy from the inside, it will positively improve your outer world. Similarly, if you have experienced something good on the outside, it will make you feel good from inside. It works like a mirror where your inner-thinking and your outer world experience reflect each other.

You must have realized this power at some point in time. You must have observed the way you think, the kind of people you meet, the type of places you visit, or the kind of things you see. This process keeps moving both from inside and outside. So, take care of your inner thinking and outside actions. Use the inner positive energy to accomplish the outer world's task and use the outer world's positive outcomes to energize your mind.

Power of Momentum

The power of momentum greatly affects your action capabilities. It works on the concept of Newton's first law of motion. It says, "Once you bring yourself in motion, then you remain in motion yourself." This power defines the importance of habits in a way. If you bring yourself in the pace of action, then you automatically accomplish your tasks.

You can also try it practically. If you want to do a particular task, but you are not able to do it. Now, get it into the momentum, and you'll be able to do it. For example, you want to read a book, but you are not finding interest in it.

Now, begin the momentum; read this for a short time. If you read this for some time, you will find your interest even for 5 to 10 minutes. Your interest will keep you in the momentum.

Repeated involvement in the process will make you more effective. More so, this is highly effective in reducing 'procrastination' problems.

Once you bring yourself in motion, you will finish one task, and then it will bring you forward to do the other task.

Power of Choice

The power of choice means that the power of selection. It reflects your authority on your own life. Only you have control over your life, and nobody can annoy you without your consent. No one else has the right to make you inferior, and no one can make you sad without your permission. Nobody is big nor small in this world. Any slavery begins in mind. You know that your mind is free, nobody else can confine it, and nobody can restrain it.

You always have the power to choose. Either you select slavery or freedom; it depends on you only. The option is like an 'on' and 'off' button for you. If you keep it 'on,' you will be the boss, and if you turn it off, you will give control to others. The powers of the mind are with you. It depends on you whether you choose to use it or lose it. If you want to bring changes in your life, you must use the power of choice.

The Power of Creativity

Creativity is a software that has the most significant contribution to the reprogramming of your mind. But now, as you know, it is the natural ability of the mind. So it is not just software, but in a way, it is more like the operating system. Once your thought process starts running in the right direction, everything becomes more comfortable for you.

The best practice of awakening the power of creativity is to use it. This power is within you. You just need to use it. Intensive thinking is the essence of creativity. Fearless, critical, or deep-thinking initiates creativity. Also, exploring new things and keeping yourself in the right direction enhances creativity. Once you indulge in creative thinking, you will see its impact in different spheres of your life. It also improves your other abilities. It will enhance your decision-making ability, and you will build a great future for yourself.

Power of Self-Acceptance

The power of acceptance is significant. Only those people who can accept themselves can transform themselves. Self-acceptance does not mean accepting yourself only when you are perfect, nor do you have to accept it as your inferior self.

It means being conscious of your strengths and weaknesses. It is to accept yourself entirely and emerge as the best version of yourself, and it is about utilizing your strengths and defusing your weaknesses. It's about believing in yourself.

The power of self-acceptance is impressive. Once it is awakened, you do not need the acceptance of others to be happy. When you recognize it, your self-image becomes surprisingly strong, and your self-esteem reaches to the highest level.

HOW TO UNLEASH THE WILLPOWER IN YOU

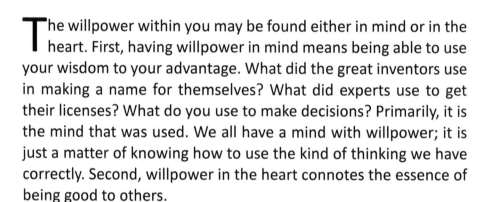

The willpower within you may be found either in mind or in the heart. First, having willpower in mind means being able to use your wisdom to your advantage. What did the great inventors use in making a name for themselves? What did experts use to get their licenses? What do you use to make decisions? Primarily, it is the mind that was used. We all have a mind with willpower; it is just a matter of knowing how to use the kind of thinking we have correctly. Second, willpower in the heart connotes the essence of being good to others.

There is no sweeter gift than seeing others smile because of you. It is our hearts that influences other people's attitudes as well as stir their emotions. Heart makes us strong and, at the same time, weak. Every time we make others happy, our hearts seem to be stronger. But when we become the reason for others' grief, we felt a certain kind of guilt that causes pain. Your heart may be your willpower; it is just a matter of discovering your angel side.

However, if not the best, it will be better when the willpower waiting to be discovered in us is both from the mind and the heart. Any person who has an educated mind and an ethical heart will never go wrong. If you can, why not try to put into action the way of thinking you have through your heart?

We are not born with the potential to bring out the willpower inside us automatically. We are born with minds, but we are not gifted with a particular magical characteristic that can grant our wildest wishes. We are born to discover how to discover things waiting to be discovered. Welcome each day with positive vibes. It is easier to manage things if you started your day with a smile, a genuine smile. A positive start will lead you to a good end. Being motivated from the very first hour of the day will keep you going for the whole twenty-four hours. Never let negative things ruin what you have started. Smile at a problem so that the problem will smile at you. Be happy for every second of the day.

Learn from your mistakes. We are human beings who are prone to committing mistakes. Mistakes are normal, but committing mistakes every now and then is not. Mistakes should never be repeated because you must learn from them. When you already knew that mishandling knives would make you bleed, then do not try it again. If you get the illustration point on the knife, you know that a mistake is a once in a lifetime experience. Mistakes are supposed to be past lessons, and past lessons are supposed to be learned. Oversee the best in you. Never underestimate yourself. Never feel that you are inferior because no one is. We are all born naked, which means that we are all equal.

The only person who has the power to make you less of a person is you alone. Always look at the best in you and motivate others to do the same. While looking for the best in you, do not forget to also look at others' best things. In that way, you will be able just to appreciate each other. Of course, criticisms are normal. You can actually criticize yourself for failure. However, such criticism must be a constructive one.

Criticisms are intended to develop yourself and not to make you feel less worthy.

Winners never quit. Always be motivated. Do not let the word ‚give up' occupy your vocabulary. Winners fail, but they never quit. Keep going on until you achieve what you have been longing for. Winners are those who, despite too much failure and discouragements, still managed to stand up and be back on track. Life is not a game; as a result, you cannot quit. Life is more than engaging in a game where your only choice is to win.

Relax because everything will be fine. Since you started the day with positive vibes, end it with a smile. Inhale the good things which happened during the day and exhale the negative ones. You deserve a break. We all deserve it. Look back and assume that you had a great day, and you deserve enough sleep so that tomorrow, you will again welcome your day with positive vibes.

It is your responsibility to share your knowledge with other people. Do not be selfish; no one succeeds in being selfish. How to share willpower? Teach, give back, and inspire are the answers. Teach. Learning comes with teaching. Teach others the lessons you learned in your life. Teach them how to bring out the best inside them. Teach them how to discover their inner willpower. If they fail, never get tired of teaching them. Be persistent in making them believe that people have an innate character that will help them reach the goals they wished for.

Give back. Have a kind heart. Thank everything who have helped you one way or the other in achieving your goals. The phrase ‚giving back' means doing good things for others because the world has been good to you. There is no other better feeling than to see another smile because of you. We are humans. We can never be equal in terms of money or fame. But we are humans who can put into external acts the true essence of equality. Treat others as if they have done concrete good things for you; in that way, you will ultimately feel how much people value you.

Inspire. Make the story of your life an avenue for other people to believe that everything is possible. Inspiring others is being honest. Disclose everything; all your ups and downs. One person who was inspired because of you will contribute a positive change in the society. What more if you will be able to inspire hundreds or thousands?

Willpower is a circular pattern, not linear. You can insert any good thing in between. What you did from the start will lead you to the last, and the last will lead you to the beginning. Continue inspiring yourself as well as the others.

KEY POINTERS FOR SUCCESS

Try to Minimize the Tyranny of Negative Thoughts

It is important to remember to focus our efforts on becoming self-aware to recognize and recognize quickly when becoming incredibly self-critical. That way, we can act quickly to counteract the negativity.

Don't Try to Be Perfect

We can become paralyzed or demoralized by the assumption that we have to succeed in whatever we try, succeed in, and succeed well. Few of us achieve absolute perfection in our endeavors that if we think we always have to aim for it, we will be setting ourselves up to fail. To move forward, we have to settle for 'aim high, but aim realistically.'

View Mistakes as Learning Opportunities

If we are to keep a high level of self-esteem, we have to accept that we will make mistakes because that's part of life – we try something, make a mistake, hopefully, learn from it, and move forward by trying again. A child doesn't learn to walk without ever falling over. Given that our learning capacity continues throughout our lives, the mistakes will keep on happening as we continue the learning journey. If we choose to see them negatively as problems, then our self-esteem will continue to be challenged at every step. But if we see them positively as opportunities, then we are more likely to embrace them rather than feel threatened by them.

Try New Things

Where self-esteem is low, we can fall into the trap of protecting our fragile self-image from a further threat by not putting ourselves out there for testing, as it were. If we have been preyed to painful criticism or ridicule in the past, we may not want to risk this happening again if we don't perform well. It is a perfectly reasonable fear in such circumstances, but we're always the bystander; we do not allow ourselves to challenge that negative self-image. What if it turns out that we're great at this new thing – wouldn't that be a significant boost to our self-esteem! Of course, we might be right on some occasions – that we are indeed rubbish at it – but, armed with our best positive reinforcement strategy of choice, we can move on to the other challenge without convincing ourselves that we are rubbish at everything.

As with all new endeavors, there is a risk involved, but if we don't take that risk, we might never discover new talents or interests that hold the great positive potential to enrich our lives and raise our self-esteem.

Accept Our Limitations

We have talked a lot about making changes and accepting challenges, but some things can't be changed. For example, if our eyesight is very poor, then, realistically, we're unlikely ever to become an airline pilot. If we don't accept such limitations, we may be setting ourselves up for disappointments, which can seriously affect our self-esteem.

Set Goals

Sometimes we know we have a problem with low self-esteem, but we don't have the confidence, energy, or skills to do much about it. Having a plan can make all the difference in moving us from wishing something would happen to make it happen. We might need to change that plan if the chosen strategy isn't working, but not having a plan at all means that we don't even know what we're aiming for, let alone whether we're succeeding in achieving it! And setbacks can be easier to negotiate and bounce back from if we have a plan to ground us and help us keep our vision of a more self-assured and confident us insight. Having a role model can be helpful too, in the sense that it can remind us that success is achievable even though the road to it might be a hard one and that others have faced difficult times and overcome the odds.

Make Quality' Me' Time

If we have low self-esteem, we often fail to gift ourselves enough personal time and space. Even if we convince ourselves that it would be in our interests, it can be not easy to find time to spend on ourselves and our own needs. So, instead of trying to find the time, we need to make that time. Even ten minutes each day to concentrate on feeling confident and assured can be enough. And we need to do it not because we have been told to, but because we have enough self-esteem to tell our- selves that we deserve it.

Act Confident

Let's act confidently, even if we don't feel confident inside. Some people are likely to assume that we are and to engage with us accordingly – complimenting us, offering us opportunities for advancement, and so on. The more this occurs, the more likely we are to start believing their assumption that we are confident and actually to be confident, rather than having to act confident. Consequently, we are likely to find it easier to move into new encounters with confidence because our self-esteem will have grown as a result of the positive experience.

Do Something We're Good At

Although it is essential to try new things to address problems, if self-esteem is low, it can help concentrate on getting better at what we're good at before tackling something we fear or are not so good at. Suppose we face a challenge with our self- esteem at a high level because we have recently experienced success or a sense of achievement somehow. In that case, we are likely to do better with the new challenge than if we had approached it already doubting that we could ever succeed.

Commend Ourselves for Trying

Sometimes, if we don't get to the top of the metaphorical hill we have set ourselves to climb, we consider ourselves to have failed. If our self-esteem is not to be regularly shattered, we need to praise ourselves for effort as well as achievement – that is, for even getting started on the hill climb, even if we never actually make it right to the top. If we can get on top, then all to the good, but if we see that as the only measure of success, then we are likely to know every stumble along the way as a failure. To be blinded of the bigger picture in which we are moving steadily onward and upward despite setbacks along the way.

Make Progress Look Achievable

The bigger picture might seem daunting when our self-esteem is low, but it will appear less daunting if it can be 'knocked down to size' by the breaking down of big goals into smaller and more specific aims – each small step being part of a bigger journey. The broad goal of having high self-esteem may well seem beyond our reach, and any progress difficult to chart. But when divided into smaller steps, the charting (and celebrating) of success becomes much easier, and the likelihood of that ultimate goal being reached optimized.

Embrace Self-Determination

We have seen that factors other than our own desires come into play when enhancing our self-esteem. For example, suppose we are subject to discrimination for some reason. In that case, our chances of successfully raising our self-esteem may be hampered by the power of negative stereotyping to convince ourselves and others that we are (and should be) at the bottom of the pile in terms of being worthy members of the human race. However, while the journey towards high self-esteem may be easier for some than others, those with the strongest sense of self-determination will be the ones most likely to succeed. We do not have to have self-belief at the beginning of the journey, but we both want to change and believe that we can. With a belief in self-determination, the transformation can begin.

CONCLUSION

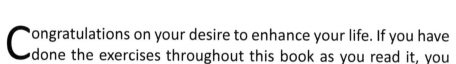

Congratulations on your desire to enhance your life. If you have done the exercises throughout this book as you read it, you are well on your way toward self-acceptance and self- confidence for a fulfilled life.

Many people ask whether it is success or failure that teaches you the most significant lessons in life. It is both, but only when you take the time to self-reflect and learn from the experience. Even if you had great success, it might be hard to replicate it in the future if you didn't self-reflect to know what went right versus what was luck. The same is true with a mistake. Unless you self-reflect on what occurred, you are likely to keep repeating the same mistake. Many people don't like to do the work that self-reflection requires because they either want to celebrate or sulk. They don't realize that when self-reflection is done properly, they will always have something to celebrate. We encourage you to remember this moving forward, as this is the first step that will lead you to a fulfilled life.

This book was written from experience and positioned as a way to repair years of self-doubt, frustration, and lack of confidence. It is great that resources such as this and many other helpful books exist. However, the ideal situation would be to teach this art of self-acceptance and self-confidence in childhood so that all humans can live a fulfilled life from the beginning. Therefore, if you are blessed to have children or have a child in your life, you can mentor, teach them this at a young age. Raise them this way. Honestly, this book was written for people who had to learn this mid-life. But it should also be a book for youth, so they naturally do this throughout their lives and have it mastered by the time they are in their forties and fifties. Instead of relearning it or learning it for the first time at that age when they are fighting so many other uphill battles.

As you complete this book, our desire for you is that you remember the importance of all these steps. Always give yourself the time to self-reflect, forgive, and grow and learn from every big incident in your life. It is also important to remember your innate curiosity for all that is around you and to be grateful. The more you live in these moments of learning and growing and being curious, the more comfortable you will feel to show your beautifully courageous self. Learning from your experiences, reflecting and growing from it, there is nothing that will stand in your way and slow you down.

If it helps you to journal throughout this time, develop a healthy routine in your life so you can make the time for it. Journaling enables you to remember the high highs and low lows, stay on track, and continually learn and grow. Whenever you can pass your learnings and experiences on to another person, do so. Sharing your experience not only helps that person grow but enables you to grow as well. When you share something, it puts you in a teaching position, and that teaching allows you to remember the message more deeply. If you are interested in starting journaling but don't know where to start, a natural starting point would be writing your values definitions.

Eventually, you worry about yourself since you cannot change another person. You can try hard to influence, but you cannot change them. Throughout your journey, you can try to bring others along with you. If they come, that is fantastic. If they don't, you must let it go. Not everyone in this world is ready for this type of work. Sometimes you see divorces, years of friendship dissolving or people no longer talking to their family members because heavy work like this needed to happen, and one side was ready for it, and the other was not. Better say a prayer for them, wish them well, and let it go. Part of the prayer is for them to realize the importance of doing this hard work to become deeply fulfilled individuals.

Self-acceptance occurs once you know yourself. You get to know yourself deeply when you self-reflect on your actions, beliefs, and encounters. That self-reflection will uncover good, bad, and indifferent feelings that you will need to evaluate to learn and grow from it. Some of those lessons may require forgiveness of yourself and others. Forgiveness releases your heart. With a light heart that is not heavy with burdens, you can identify what you value in life. These values support you and your life decisions, making opportunities clearer and choices more comfortable with driving. With this support, you can see life through a positive lens that makes you grateful for your life and all the people and situations in it. With this optimistic outlook on life, you become curious about all that might be possible for you. As you explore these curiosities and have won under your belt, you become courageous.

Using the lessons and successes you have had up to this point, you should continue to grow and learn and pass these experiences on to others to help them in their lives. Throughout this process, you will grow more confident and feel fulfilled because you live a beautiful life.

Lightning Source UK Ltd.
Milton Keynes UK
UKHW022256301120
374378UK00005B/836